D0103831

9/11

9/11

THE CULTURE OF COMMEMORATION

David Simpson

The University of Chicago Press

CHICAGO & LONDON

The University of Chicago Press, Chicago 60637
The University of Chicago Press, Ltd., London
© 2006 by The University of Chicago
All rights reserved. Published 2006
Printed in the United States of America

15 14 13 12 11 10 09 08 07   5 4 3 2

ISBN (cloth): 0-226-75938-5
ISBN (paper): 0-226-75939-3

Library of Congress Cataloging-in-Publication Data

Simpson, David, 1951–
     9/11 : the culture of commemoration / David Simpson.
        p.   cm.
     Includes bibliographical references (p.   ) and index.
     ISBN 0-226-75938-5 (cloth : acid-free paper) —
     ISBN 0-226-75939-3 (pbk. : acid-free paper)
     1. September 11 Terrorist Attacks, 2001—Influence.
   2. September 11 Terrorist Attacks, 2001—Anniversaries, etc.
   3. Memorials—Philosophy.   4. Critical theory.
   I. Title: Nine/eleven.   II. Title.
   HV6432.7.S557   2006
   973.931—dc22
                                                    2005024418

Long after we are all gone, it's the sacrifice of our patriots and their heroism that is going to be what this place is remembered for.

RUDOLPH GIULIANI

But why do they need to be called "heroes"? Perhaps this word has different connotations in American English than it does in German.

JÜRGEN HABERMAS

Contents

Acknowledgments

I thank Mary-Kay Wilmers and the editorial staff at the *London Review of Books* for the hospitality of their columns to early drafts of material appearing here in chapters 1 and 3; and Julian Hunt for encouraging me to write about the plans for rebuilding the World Trade Center site in Lower Manhattan. What I wrote for him has not been published, but some of it appears in chapter 2. Alan Thomas at the University of Chicago Press has been exceptionally helpful with every stage of this project. I was fortunate to have two readers who gave uncommonly detailed attention to the manuscript. One of them, W. J. T. Mitchell, read it twice. He gave me a rigorous and unsparing critique of an early and untimely draft, and hugely improved what came later, which he also read with an energy and imagination for which I am deeply grateful. I am also indebted to a second reader, who offered several pages of meticulous suggestions that became more and more useful to me as I read and reread them. In particular, any success I have had in adjusting my own rhetoric away from inhabiting the same assumed consensus about "proper" memorialization that I am critiquing owes much to this reader's report. My colleague Catherine Robson has been a constant source of stimulus and suggestion on the topic of death and commemoration, and I have learned much from her own related project on unburied bodies. Conversations with Scott Shershow have both sharpened my argument and extended my sense of what I needed to read. Among others who have responded to my queries or offered helpful insights and information, I thank Ian Beckett, David Clark, Billy Kelly, Sharon Oster, Tim Morton, and Harry Richardson. I also thank Susanna Ferguson for typing the bibliography with speed and accuracy. Mary Anne Ferguson read the whole manuscript closely and helpfully; Margaret Ferguson read several versions of everything and made, as always, important intellectual contributions throughout.

I feel lucky to be able once again to acknowledge the love, insight, and support of Margaret Ferguson and of our three children.

Introduction

Taking Time

The whole play of history and power is disrupted by
this event, but so, too, are the conditions of analysis.
You have to take your time

JEAN BAUDRILLARD,
The Spirit of Terrorism and Requiem for the Twin Towers

Has the world changed since 9/11? If it has, then in what ways? If it
has not changed, then who has an interest in claiming that it has?
Whose world are we talking about? Acts of commemoration are
particularly sensitive occasions for assessing the balance of change
and continuity within the culture at large. They often declare their
adherence to time-honored and even universally human rituals
and needs, but nothing is more amenable to political and commercial manipulation than funerals, monuments, epitaphs, and obituaries. Outpourings of communal or national grief are proposed as
spontaneous but are frequently stage-managed: Abraham Lincoln's
funeral train made carefully scheduled and choreographed stops
on its protracted twelve-day passage from Washington, D.C., to
Springfield, Illinois, in the sad spring of 1865.

Commemorative practices are themselves composed of elements
that seem deeply traditional and repetitive, along with others that
are open to innovation and surprise. Still others appear to be
enduring but can be related to long-term historical preferences that
shift slowly but shift nonetheless. Grieving over and laying to rest
the bodies of the dead, summarizing and remembering their lives in
obituaries and epitaphs, and erecting monuments and buildings
that memorialize or mark the sites of tragic events have all been
part of the rituals of ongoing life, but not always in the same way or
to the same ends. In the period of the modern nation-states, these
events have taken on national significance when the occasion has

seemed to demand it.[1] In these same states, millions have died in designated pursuit of national-political ambitions and in avowed defense of homelands. Their deaths have generally been emphatically pronounced worthwhile, not to have been in vain: motherlands, fatherlands, and fellow citizens have celebrated the sacrifices and observed the endings with dignity and ceremony. If all of this has taken on a certain familiar quality, as evident, for example, on the battlefields at Waterloo, Gettysburg, or the Somme, it has remained the case that for those immediately affected, the families and friends of the dead, every death is horribly immediate and unrepeatable. Rituals of memorialization exist to assimilate these intense and particular griefs into received vocabularies and higher, broader realms than the merely personal. The routines of commemorative culture, whether private or public, exist to mediate and accommodate the unbearably dissonant agonies of the survivors into a larger picture that can be metaphysical or national-political and is often both at once. They must somehow signify and acknowledge the idiosyncrasies and special qualities of each of the dead, so that each death is not simply merged with innumerable others, without allowing those idiosyncrasies to disturb or radically qualify the comforting articulation of a common cause and a common fate. In public memorials the personal identification may be nothing more than a name on a wall, but it is still intended and felt as personal.

Taking physical leave of the dead, when there is a body to inter or cremate, normally happens soon after death, and usually with some premeditated ceremony combining tradition and deliberate personalization. Decisions about the monumental, public forms that commemorate local or national traumas and tragedies are often and ideally the products of slow time. The Vietnam Veterans Memorial in Washington, D.C., was not built until seven years after the end of a war that proved too divisive and unresolved to allow for ready representation; the World War II Memorial took form even more belatedly, not so much because its memories are divisive (though some of them are that) but because its scope was so great

---

1. Benedict Anderson began his influential study of modern nationalisms with some comments on death and on the symptomatic power of tombs of unknown soldiers; see Anderson, *Imagined Communities: Reflections on the Origins and Spread of Nationalism,* rev. ed. (London and New York: Verso, 1991), 9–12.

as to seem beyond representation at all, except as a series of relatively local events: hence the monuments at Pearl Harbor (another memorial that was a long time coming), to the Iwo Jima flag raising, and to the Bataan death march, among others. Holocaust memorials also came late, and are still coming, for a range of reasons that include national and international shame or embarrassment and a sense of iconographic inadequacy (how can it be represented?) as well as of unsolved histories and contested contemporary politics. A culture that can *take* time over the commemoration of its past signals in its protracted deliberations the expectation that it will *have* time, that it can look forward to a continuous future both in the minimal sense of mere survival and in the more substantial sense that events from the past will be explained and set into context, made part of an intelligible history. But there is often a sense of guilt or unease that accompanies the assumption of an ongoing history with its implicit emphasis on coming to terms with and getting over tragic events. This is particularly so since the last quarter of the twentieth century, the period of the so-called memory boom, when a proper acknowledgment of the enormity of human cruelty (typified by and sometimes limited to the Nazi genocide) has often seemed to insist that we not pass into a future that is forgetful of the history of atrocity, even that we reenact the primary shock of suffering itself as a state not to be overcome but endlessly made present. This has led to a besetting sense of bad faith about both forgetting (as if we could, but we do) *and* remembering (as if we could suffer in any way as much as those who lived and died in the camps). Freud's brief remarks on the distinction between mourning and melancholia, getting over (working through) and acting out, have proved hugely prophetic of and influential for late twentieth-century deliberations on the ethical and psychological burdens of a horrific past.[2] Above all, what has been deemed most intolerable is the role of the bystander, the person who simply notices but does not act. At the same time

---

2. Exemplary here is the work of Dominick LaCapra, who has sought to recommend a middle way between the traumatic arrest of acting out and the potentially glib comforts of too easily working through; see, especially, LaCapra, *Representing the Holocaust: History, Theory, Trauma* (Ithaca, NY: Cornell University Press, 1994), 205–23; and idem, *History and Memory after Auschwitz* (Ithaca, NY: Cornell University Press, 1998), 95–138.

the inhabitants of affluent countries, whose economic position insulates them from the routine sight of violence, are often just that, bystanders, biding their time.

The event of September 11, 2001, seemed to challenge such complacency. It has been widely presented as an interruption of the deep rhythms of cultural time, a cataclysm simply erasing what was there rather than evolving from anything already in place, and threatening a yet more monstrous future. It appeared as an unforeseen eruption across the path of a history commonly deemed rooted in a complacent steady-state progressivism (the well-known "end of history" mooted after the fall of the Soviet empire). The forms of its commemoration have been correspondingly urgent and perhaps untimely hurried along and even hijacked by a tide of secondary events whose connections with 9/11 are to say the least open to dispute. In less than two years we went from the fall of the Twin Towers and the attack on the Pentagon to the invasion of Iraq, a process marked by propagandist compression and manufactured consent so audacious as to seem unbelievable, except that it happened. The time of memory and commemoration evolved from the start alongside the time of revenge, but those now being punished were not the original aggressors. Most of the world knows this and stands appalled. Political scientist Jenny Edkins has seen 9/11 as the moment when "trauma time collided with the time of the state, the time of capitalism, the time of routine," producing a "curious unknown time, a time with no end in sight." Most worrying to her is that "the state, or whatever form of power is replacing it, has taken charge of trauma time."[3] The balance between acting out and working through has been skewed by a prolonged period of ideological shoring up and military hitting out. Mourning and melancholia have both been made secondary to the initiation of new states of emergency. For a national culture as committed as is that of the United States to a high level of ethical self-justification and even self-righteousness, this compression produces a definite tension in the conventions of national self-representation. If the ethical task is somehow to "know how to reinstate justice in the place of vengeance," then it requires (and has produced) a radically devious

3. Jenny Edkins, *Trauma and the Memory of Politics* (Cambridge: Cambridge University Press, 2003), 233.

logic to justify the invasion of Iraq.[4] In the face of this deviance it is tempting to agree with Badiou that 9/11 and the "following battles" represent little more than the *"disjunctive synthesis of two nihilisms"* (158).

The dissemination of a war *against* terror has depended on a locution full of historical and contemporary ironies, for terror began its lexical life as the policy of the state, and wars are traditionally waged by states, so the war against terror can be (and has been) deciphered as the war of the state against itself. But international events are not the only sources of interruption of or distraction from the working out of memorial vocabularies for the dead of 9/11. There is also the ongoing negotiation between commerce and commemoration at the WTC site, a process that pits the declared obligations of memory and due respect against those of a future civic life, both economic and cultural. It is easy to cast the moguls of Manhattan as insensitive and materialistic, but the memorial process has also been aggressively suborned by the politicians, whose avowed respect for the dead is not beyond suspicions of present and future self-interest. Debates about the use of the site have not been unmarked by the assumption that the dead should bury the dead and thus by an embarrassingly hasty inclination to get on with life. Many residents have made it clear that they do not wish to live in a national memorial emptied of retail, full of tourists by day and deserted by night. On the other side, melancholic extremes can also be identified among some of the survivor families and other involved groups who want the site to remain always a shrine to the departed.

Through all of these contexts and situations, the sense of the disruptive power of 9/11 has seemed apparent. Its exceptionality has been taken to affront the sense we have of *our* culture—that *we* do not do not engage in acts of terror and have not known them. At the same time, and right from the start, there were many people who gave voice to the odd and troubling sensation that they had already seen those falling towers in the movies—movies made in America. On the one hand 9/11 has been described as the result of

4. Alain Badiou, *Infinite Thought: Truth and the Return of Philosophy*, trans. and ed. Oliver Feltham and Justin Clemens (London and New York: Continuum, 2003), 143.

a clash of civilizations, ours and theirs, signaling the existence of an implacably different culture that does not march to the same beat as ours, one that is messianic, vengeful, unenlightened, premodern, other: the culture of terror. The relatively comfortable pluralism within which we have been living, whereby other cultures have come to be accepted in their own terms as long as they subsist at some same distance from (or peacefully within) our own, was shattered by this event's confrontational negation of any ethic of tolerance. On the other hand that strangeness looked familiar, both as an image on the television or movie screen and as a massively amplified rerun of a previous attack on the same building in 1993, an event that with the wisdom of hindsight looks like part of a pattern developing through slow time, and thus very much a part of our inherited culture. That which looked to many of us, on September 11, 2001, like the work of agents so unfamiliar as to seem almost like aliens, also looked like something we had seen before in both fact and fiction.

We should then question those who have presented 9/11 as an attack on culture itself, on any meaningful continuity with the past and with a projected future. In the eyes of our enemy, they tell us, 9/11 was intended as a cataclysmic imposition of revelation and apocalypse, of eternally present time, on the complacent faith in merely historical and evolutionary temporality that characterizes our secular preference for prudence, profit, and accumulation in the world of trade, a world of self-cultivation measured by the reassuring ticking of a predictable clock. (The ticking clock was rendered radically threatening in one of the Republican Party's televised campaign ads before the election of November 2004.) Michael Ignatieff's "apocalyptic nihilism" partakes of this rhetoric, as does Thomas Friedman's description of 9/11 as a "hole in the fabric of civilization."[5] The attribution of nihilism or nothingness (despite Osama bin Laden's explicit demands for specific changes in U.S. foreign policy) creates a space for speculation and interpretation that is literally inexhaustible. In the light of this construction of nothing, of inviting emptiness, everything becomes a

---

5. Michael Ignatieff, *The Lesser Evil: Political Ethics in an Age of Terror* (Princeton: Princeton University Press, 2004), 99; Thomas L. Friedman, *Searching for the Roots of 9/11*, Discovery Channel, March 26, 2003.

possible motive: the attack may then be the result of jealousy, of "them" wanting what we have and destroying it because they cannot have it ("they hate our freedom"); or it may be the result of an absolute negation, of "them" responding to an intransigent fundamentalism wholly foreign to our professed ethic of tolerance; or it may stem from "them" being too technologically undeveloped and/or cowardly to face their enemy in open combat. *They* are secretive, cowardly, primitive, inflexible: terrorists, followers of Islam. *We* are an open society, honorable, sophisticated, and committed to the global conversation and to respectful dialogue. We stand up in place and identify ourselves; they are anonymous and everywhere.] - *what?*

All of these binaries have been, from the first, disputed both as ideological figments and as empirical facts. The pilots of the hijacked planes were trained in U.S. flight schools, educated in Western ways, and were competent practitioners of Western technologies. The Osama bin Laden who is now our enemy was once our friend, as was the Saddam Hussein who was thereafter called an apostle of evil, despite there being no credible evidence of mass destructive or terrorist intentions or capacities. The everyday assumptions about the neatness of rhetorically declared oppositions, them and us, create a climate for the blatant political manipulation of binaries of the sort we have been seeing since 9/11. The passage from one entity to an unrelated other—from Osama to Saddam—under the guise of "enemy" follows a traditional logic of scapegoating at the service of a ruthlessly presentist political opportunism. It has been analyzed consistently both by anthropologists and by those who speak for what is called theory: the work of Derrida, Baudrillard, Žižek, and others should now more than ever be urgently recognized precisely in the light of popular counterclaims by both left and right that the project of theory has run out of time, gone bad, turned away from life. The repression of theory itself in its conventional appearance of foreignness and hostile rhetorical difficulty is one mark of the willed ignorance maintained by the major media inside the United States, and by many among its intelligentsia, about what the rest of the world thinks of *us*.

The history happening now has put radical pressure on the domestic humanist project of encouraging sympathy for others by way of shared feelings. The pursuit of a war against innocent people and the apparent tolerance of avoidable deaths (our own and those of others) suggest that we have *not* after all learned to suffer with others by way of a common sensing of the vulnerable body. Not yet. The sufficiency of the humanist subject as the site of ethical and aesthetic judgments, still I think the foundation of conventional intellectual work, has been visibly in question through the last four years. Nor can it convincingly be deemed ready and waiting to emerge as an adequate vehicle of just behavior if only we could remove some temporary impediments: media culture, for example, with its saturation of images and simulacra, or short-term political ideology. Edward Said's call for a humanism that is "democratic, open to all classes and backgrounds," that is not limited to "extolling patriotically the virtues of our culture, our language, our monuments," that can recognize in culture not an inert heritage but a "seething discordance of unresolved notations" and make something of them, has yet to find its audience.[6] Indeed, Said's call for a return to a "philological-interpretive model" (34) and a "*para-doxal* mode of thought" (83) will look to many persons exactly like the very same theory to which what is familiarly called humanism, in its reliance on common sense and assumed consensus, has so often been opposed. Said was never a domestic intellectual, and his humanism is itself a foreign legacy, embodied in Auerbach and Spitzer and in the traditions of Islamic *ijtihad* (58). So in the light of our obvious need to learn its lessons, the return to theory (a theory that was never lost but was rather turned off) becomes more urgent than before. Because theory has been a synonym for the other, the foreign, and for the foreign that threatens to take up residence within our borders, our classrooms (everywhere and nowhere, like terror—this position has been held in some quarters for at least forty years), it is not only an alternative to but a victim of the national self-regard that is currently so dangerous an element in world politics. But in the limited but significant hospitality we have shown to theory's foreign bodies, we have preserved a contact with the other that is potentially more valuable now than ever before. Edward Said's untimely death produced an obituary of scandalous partiality in the national newspaper of record, the *New York Times.*

6. Edward Said, *Humanism and Democratic Criticism* (New York: Columbia University Press, 2004), 21, 28.

The equally untimely passing of Jacques Derrida in October 2004 produced another instance of the same (for the Jew as for the Arab), along with an appraisal describing his career as flourishing because of "an orthodoxy in which rebellion is privileged over tradition" and his writing as often "mannered and puerile, endlessly turning rebellion on itself." The final insult of this judgment was that Derrida had the nerve to say, a propos of 9/11, that we do not yet "know what we are talking about."[7] ←

I take this remark very seriously, and as an imperative for the taking of time—that we do not yet know, most of us, what we are talking about. For, in the face of all of the nativized pressures to imagine terror as the absolute other, the enemy, the ultimate incarnation of a model of "them and us," theory has argued and is arguing for a dialectical understanding of violence and a recognition that there can be no convincing absolute distinction between us and them. Much of what nativist thinkers have dismissed as theory has been formed in the light (and shade) cast by Hegel's account of the master–slave relation in feudalism, the apparent limit-case for dialectical synthesis, as fundamentally unstable in both epistemological and historical terms: just as the master must acknowledge his own dependence on the slave in his very self-identification, so the feudal world is on its way to becoming something else, the modern, a better and becoming-better world. Theory's utopian project draws on this Hegelian sense of a recurring dialectic even as it tends to disavow progressive historicism itself, along with the belief that we are in the empirical sense already there or well along the way. Conversely, the sense of a providential narrative at work through history took on its most emphatic recent form among the apologists of free market thought after the collapse of state communism in 1989, and it has reappeared in some of the more deluded projections of the neoliberal war hawks in their talk of a "just" war. But we should hold on to Hegel's refusal to underwrite the sustainability of a strong and absolute distinction between self and other, them and us. Gil Anidjar, in a brilliant study from which I shall be drawing in some detail later in the book, has explained the "lack of integrity" of the concept of the enemy, an enemy whom we are at once to love as ourselves (according to Christian doctrine) but also

7. Edward Rothstein, "An Appraisal," New York Times, October 11, 2004, B1, 7.

to oppose as the Antichrist, an enemy who is, in the last analysis, indistinguishable from ourselves.[8]

This does not mean that there are no distinctions that matter, that there is some monolithic global culture in which all are equally implicated, like it or not, and from which all events must devolve. Global capitalism, indeed, has been taken as such, and its all-pervasive but unseen operations, for those who see it that way, make it a mirror image and perhaps a near relative of the currently projected image of terror, everywhere and nowhere. But it has not yet produced a world unmarked by significant differences and alternative ideals, though many apologists for the anglophone democracies think, after 1989, that it should and will do so. Neither do we inhabit a world of radically distinct and atomistically isolated entities, called cultures or civilizations, that preserve themselves, like undiscovered tribes in some imaginary rain forest, against any formative contacts with others. Ours is a world both reproducing and resisting a totality holding together all that it contains (or all that matters to the system), but it is not a plurality of purely separate worlds, a series of doggedly impervious societies whose self-sufficiency we will celebrate if we are romantic localists or deplore if we are enthusiastic neoliberals. To counter the model of "them *and* us" with one that claims that "they *are* us" is not good enough: neither absolute binary distinctions nor essentialist identifications describe carefully enough the situation in which we are living. What we have instead are various kinds of boundary troubles that cannot be generalized into philosophical absolutes of any kind but that reveal, on close inspection of the empirical kind, that some work is to be done in understanding the different and critical imbalances of power that govern all postulates specifying identity and difference. There has been relatively little detailed attention to the record, to the "facts": the work of Noam Chomsky stands as exemplary here even as it is almost completely ignored and un-reproduced by the mainstream media in the United States.[9] The reception of the Abu Ghraib photographs is the most recent

8. Gil Anidjar, *The Jew, the Arab: A History of the Enemy* (Stanford: Stanford University Press, 2003), 32.

9. See Noam Chomsky, *9/11* (New York: Seven Stories Press, 2002); and idem, *Power and Terror: Post 9/11 Talks and Interviews*, ed. John Junkerman and Takei Masakazu (New York and Tokyo: Seven Stories Press and Little More, 2003).

reminder that there are no absolute boundaries between them and us, just as there are no simple identities: the culture of torture, as we shall see, is among the most empirical of all instances of the fragility and instability of imagined perimeters.

Taking time for the effort at an inquiry into the culture of commemoration in the light of theory raises the question of whether there is still time, whether it is too late. The resistance to complexity (or the invention of other distracting complexities) in the political and governing classes and all too often in the major media outlets supposed to be monitoring their behavior makes it unlikely that any such analysis will come from those quarters. They do not take time. But those who would do differently and better are also under pressure. The breakneck speed with which the tragic events of 9/11 have been cashed in for the pursuit of long-meditated military adventurisms and global realignments (intended or not) must make us wonder whether taking the time for sustained reflection is still worth doing. Scholarly time looks its best when there are no critical events going on around it: then it can reflect and project and even hope to appear prescient. When things speed up, we scholars run the risk of being left behind, assimilating yesterday's news. Said's *Humanism and Democratic Criticism* calls for "longer periods of reflection" than are provided by the "headline, sound-bite format" (73–74), but this is exactly the settled expectation that has been disrupted by 9/11 itself—for who knows when and if another attack will come—and even more so by the political-communicational hyperalertness disseminated worldwide by those who are using it for their various purposes. The importance of Derrida's claim that we do not yet know what we are talking about should still be the operational faith of useful inquiry. We should remain committed, in the words of another commentator, to "untimely utterances and awkward silences," to "examining what cannot or should not be said," and to "reflecting on the conditions of sayability and the unspeakable."[10] But will there be time? There is no answer to the question. One can only hope that keeping faith with the traditions of critical reflection might somehow matter to a world that can be better than the one we have now. Art Spiegelman, in one of the

---

10. W. J. T. Mitchell, "Criticism and Crisis," *Critical Inquiry* 28, no. 2 (Winter 2002): 571.

most pertinent and provocative of all the responses to 9/11, puts it thus: "I still believe the world is ending, but I concede that it seems to be ending more slowly than I once thought . . . so I figured I'd make a book."[11] As I write, in the summer of 2005, novels, plays, and films that take 9/11 as their narrative occasion are beginning to appear; these are the products of a reflection that was not instant and at sound-bite speed. The critical products of scholarly time will also follow.

In the face of the wildly unexpected events of 9/11, it was the most familiar functions of disaster culture that were produced to assuage the popular concern, and to channel both its desire to lend a hand and its need for outrage. The massive response to the immediate Red Cross appeal for blood donations now looks like a communal urge to present the disaster as conventional, as open to the standard remedies, as belonging to a familiar genre of accidents wherein there are bodies for restoration, good deeds to be done. Less charitably, the audible relief at finding an enemy in the ranks of the Islamic other was a fallback to familiar demons for those who had failed to find that enemy in Oklahoma City and again later in the investigation of the anthrax scare. When the system is in shock, it is the familiar (both good and bad) that comes first to mind and first to hand. Culture is about habit: that is its virtue as well as its limitation. Hegel (theorist extraordinaire) described "habit"—which, as *Gewohnheit,* assimilates itself to "dwelling," to *wohnen*—as at once freeing the soul from rational self-monitoring, leaving it open to being otherwise occupied and engaged with the new, while also committing it to a realm of unfreedom, to the uncritical replication of what has been given or handed down. He makes us ask whether we can have one without the other. Habit is a "being-at-home-with-oneself" that is foundational for our sanity, but it leaves us open to freedom only by marking us as already slaves of preformation.[12] Culture too is a habit that gives us the self-identity to keep going and to invent new culture while always threatening to limit us to the pure replication of a previous or imaginary wholeness; this last is the mandate of the

11. Art Spiegelman, introduction to *In the Shadow of No Towers* (New York: Pantheon, 2004).

12. G. W. F. Hegel, *Philosophy of Mind,* trans. William Wallace and A. V. Miller (Oxford: Clarendon Press, 1971), 139–47.

purely conservative. Habit has an exploratory and liberating function because it allows us to take for granted a state of affairs that we
do not have to wrestle with or constantly re-create: this is the "distraction" (*Zerstreuung*), the taking for granted or at best "casual
noticing," that Walter Benjamin hoped to see embodied in culture as
the great hope of socialist cinema, art, and architecture.[13] But the
life completely given over in the positive sense to casual notice or
distraction would be the sign of an achieved utopia, one in which
nothing new or challenging needed to come up, in which distribution had indeed undone excess and each would have enough, and
no more. We are more familiar with the negative incarnation of distraction as the figure of ideology, which presents profound habit as
an inertia open to exploitation, refurbishing our worst traditions as
guides to the future.

The event we call 9/11 has a past that we can rediscover, a present that we must monitor, and a future we can project. Many of us
who were addressing even the most circumscribed of publics—our
students or fellow academics—felt the urge, in the immediate aftermath of September 11, 2001, to make a statement, to testify, to register a response, to initiate some sort of commemoration. Many of
those responses took the form of grief, sorrow, shock, and above all,
self-recrimination at the appearance of carrying on as before. The
rhetoric veered wildly between sympathy and self-importance—as
if it were a moral duty that each of us should speak—but what was
notable was the need to register awareness of some sort. Many people all across America, not only those who knew one of the dead or
knew someone who knew someone, reported feelings of acute personal anxiety and radical insecurity, but there was never a point at
which this response could be analyzed as prior to or outside of its
mediation by television and by political manipulation. With the passage of time it may come to appear that 9/11 did not blow away our
past in an eruption of the unimaginable but that it refigured that
past into patterns open to being made into new and often dangerous
forms of sense. Take the date itself. There is now evidence that it
was not selected with absolute foresight as both the national emergency telephone number (911) and the anniversary of various

---

13. Walter Benjamin, *Selected Writings*, vol. 3: *1935–38*, ed. Michael Jennings
(Cambridge: Harvard University Press, 2002), 119–20.

momentous other events in the history of the West and its "others," but fastened on late in the planning process as the best conjunction of all sorts of pressures and conditions, some of them short term.[14] But when we rediscover those events, the prospect of a certain paranoid coherence emerges: the assassination of Allende on September 11, 1973; the British Mandate in Palestine on September 11, 1922; the U.S. invasion of Honduras on September 11, 1919; and the defeat of the Ottoman armies before the gates of Vienna on September 11, 1683. If this is not metaphysical irony or the mark of some devilish and well-informed intelligence, then it is a sign that our culture is saturated with such coincidences, that almost *any* date would bring up other anniversaries, any of which could become significant in the light of a supervening event. Take September 10, the date of John Smith's assumption of the presidency of the Jamestown colony (1608), or of the beginning of the British economic boycott of Iran (1951). Or take September 12, the date of the first major U.S. offensive in Europe (1918), or of the defeat of Persia by Athens at the battle of Marathon (490 BCE), or of the birth of Richard Gatling, inventor of the Gatling gun (1818). These dates are not quite as redolent with significance as that of September 11, but they are not without significance. September 12 comes up on various Internet searches as the beginning of an era, the "September 12 era"; for one webmaster the date is the "ongoing reminder" of the "positive emotions" we are all deemed to have experienced. Fortuitously the FBI attack on the Branch Davidian compound in Waco, Texas, took place on April 19, 1993—Patriots' Day. So too therefore it was on April 19, 1995, that Timothy McVeigh detonated his bomb in Oklahoma City.[15]

These are examples of how an event supposedly without precedent draws to itself a new history and projects a new future, a culture past, present, and to come. Some of these inventions are immediate, but they draw on traditional resources that are indispensable even as they are felt to be inadequate. As we ponder the

14. There is evidence that the attacks were postponed at least twice, with the hijackers finally buying tickets for September 11 only between August 25 and September 5. See *The 9/11 Commission Report*, official government ed., photographic reprint (Baton Rouge: Claitor Publishing, 2004), 248–53.

15. See Edward T. Linenthal, *The Unfinished Bombing: Oklahoma City in American Memory* (New York and Oxford: Oxford University Press, 2001), 6.

appropriate means by which to commemorate and memorialize the dead, we are engaging with an element of culture that perhaps goes back to the proverbial dawn of civilization, if the ritualized burying of the dead is indeed to be imagined (as Vico imagined it) as that which makes humans something other than beasts. And as we witness the effort to rebuild at the purposively designated "Ground Zero" what has been brought down and listen to the arguments about it, we are participating in a process of seeking to harmonize the need for shelter and commemoration with the desire for display and political advantage that has governed all public and much other building since buildings came onto the human scene. The massive national debate about memory and memorialization in relation to history has the potential to reinvigorate a debate about these issues that previously had been focused on the Holocaust and had before 9/11 been widely felt to be approaching its exhaustion. Or perhaps the debate will fizzle and falter so that the final pieces of the site plan in New York will slip into place almost unnoticed beyond the parameters of Lower Manhattan. Pierre Nora's encyclopedic *Realms of Memory* set out to produce for modern France a site-based cultural record that was premised on the end of authentic memory, of a world in which "memory is a real part of everyday experience," and the onset of a society entirely driven by responding to the "thin film of current events."[16] This elegiac paradigm pitted memory against history, the one sacred and the other critically demystifying. The "sites of memory" (lieux de mémoire) he records are themselves only vestiges of a lost integrity, the products of "a society fundamentally absorbed by its own transformation and renewal" (6). Nora's own gathering of critical instances is itself selective and can be read as a somewhat willful construction of accepted vestiges; it falls prey to the motivations of an inevitable

16. Pierre Nora, *Realms of Memory: Rethinking the French Past*, vol. 1: *Conflicts and Divisions*, ed. Lawrence D. Kritzman, trans. Arthur Goldhammer (New York: Columbia University Press, 1996), 1–2. The literature on memory is of course vast. I mention only two other items here: Yosef Hayim Yerushalmi, *Zakhor: Jewish History and Jewish Memory* (Seattle: University of Washington Press, 1982), which asks important questions about the substitution of memory for history; and Paul Ricoeur, *Memory, History, Forgetting*, trans. Kathleen Blamey and David Pellauer (Chicago: University of Chicago Press, 2004), a magisterial analysis of the relations between ethics, testimony, history, and individual and social memory.

historiography. So too will the vestiges of 9/11, whatever they turn out to be.

The need and desire for critique therefore remains unembarrassed. The commemoration of 9/11, and 9/11's culture of commemoration, has both history and a future. The event has been and will be made to mark a new epoch, and as such it is already generating a mythology and a set of practices of its own. This process is not autonomous but, precisely, *cultured,* in the sense of cultivated, and monitored and produced with the specific possibilities of consumption in mind. The event known as 9/11 lives on as the emergency telephone number painted on the sides of thousands of police cars, fire trucks, and ambulances, a part of our communications rhetoric of which one suspects that some of the hijackers were quite aware, even if the choice of this date was for them a matter of chance. It remains an emergency condition, not just because of the disaster itself (already drummed into our visual imaginations as a flat-screen phenomenon that is repetitively seen while it cannot be "imagined") and its potential recurrence in some other American place (against which homeland security is trying to protect us), but as the available icon of a massive reorganization of the global political sphere on the principles of U.S. exceptionalism and unilateralism—a reorganization that is ongoing and widely held, elsewhere in the world, to be extremely dangerous. What the term *9/11* actually names, as Jacques Derrida was quick to point out in the weeks following the event, is critically unclear. Who first coined the phrase, and how did it spread so quickly across the airwaves and into the lexicon? We may never know the answer—things happened so fast, abbreviation seemed the only way to go. The figure 9/11 is not a place (although New York City plays that role in the national imaginary), nor yet even a time, since what is missing is the designation of the year, 2001. It will repeat itself every year, and it will remain an open designation, a communications channel for crisis, an emergency number. At one moment these numbers will be a sign of remembering the dead, at another the mandate for military adventurism, at yet another an architectural and civic opportunity. The slimmed-down economy of this signifier can draw to itself, with minimum resistance, almost anything that comes its way— and anything that is sent in its direction. The power of its manipulable iconicity is such that the Bush White House can repetitively at once affirm and deny that there is evidence linking Saddam Hussein to the attack on the World Trade Towers, even where there isn't any, confident that many Americans will continue to believe that such a connection exists, a view continually reinforced by images of falling towers and statements that the war in Iraq is about fighting "terrorism" in the open and in a contained place rather than having to respond to its sinister and untraceable penetration of the world system and of the homeland in particular. Alternatively, 9/11 is deployed in the telescoping of an entire worldwide threat syndrome into the living rooms of each and all of us. Army National Guard recruiting literature delivered to my high-school age daughter in April 2004 began with the headline "The Most Important Weapon in the War on Terrorism . . . You."

In arguing that the culture of 9/11 has a longer history than many have supposed, even as we must recognize its disruptive forms, my inquiry takes very long views—of the culture of epitaphs, obituaries, and of the naming of the dead, of the building of the shelter and the monument—and relatively short views (though with long-term implications)—the framing of the dead, the war in Iraq, the rebuilding at "Ground Zero." Language itself is a major resource in the naming of what cannot be named, in the location of 9/11 within the longstanding rituals and short-term political strategies that it embodies and enables: so we have *sacred ground, Ground Zero,* the *heroes* of 9/11, the careening hyperbole that shifted from *shock and awe* to *infinite justice* to *enduring freedom* to the *Freedom Tower* itself. All of these terms, and others like them, have already been naturalized and pass by without question in the national media and the popular imagination. The normalization of these terms within the standard lexicon so that they can be repeated without question is precisely one of the most effective ways in which culture is remade. No responsible intellectual should fail to notice and respond to this process.

Much has already been written about 9/11 and its effects on political theory, foreign policy, and legal procedure.[17] For some of the reasons I have already invoked, the consequences for culture are being assessed at a slower pace. A cynical observer might have predicted that the notoriously voracious apparatus of cultural studies or cultural

---

17. See, for example, the bibliography given in Ignatieff, *Lesser Evil,* 171–72.

criticism would have been as quick to respond to the disaster as were those rescue workers who answered the call on that terrible day. This has not happened, not yet. We have had lots of memoirs, documentary records, political and legal debates, but rather less in the way of cultural analysis. This is only just beginning; it takes time, as it is about time. It is not ready and waiting for modification and discussion, the way a constitution is, or a legal scenario. It is not printed up in summary form or contained in a series of precedents that can be readily accessed. It is, taken seriously, nothing less than everything, but we cannot talk about everything at once. The event of 9/11 has both reproduced and refigured culture, which means that it may take more time than usual to work out how and to what ends. One beginning can be made by attending to the culture of commemoration.

In chapter 1, "Remembering the Dead," I place the modes of remembrance that sprang up in the immediate aftermath of 9/11 into a tradition of mourning and commemoration that both gives life to and contrasts with what happened in the last months of 2001 in America. The convergence of the dissemination of the *New York Times*'s hugely popular "Portraits of Grief" series with a truncated and complicated mourning process (few bodies or body parts, an immediately politicized rhetoric of remembrance) produced a symptomatically resonant kind of obituary that deserves close attention. If the burial of the dead is indeed a foundational ritual in human cultures, then 9/11 has taken that ritual in new directions. Chapter 2, "The Tower and the Memorial," takes up the debates around and prospects for a new architectural configuration at Ground Zero, one that is torn between tragedy and triumphalism, between remembering the dead and celebrating the political credo of the American way of life. The seemingly now-accepted hyperbole of the Freedom Tower looks set to coexist with the starker subterranean environment of the memorial in a juxtaposition that registers a more general uncertainty about what 9/11 means and for whom it means. In chapter 3, "Framing the Dead," I discuss the aftermath of the culture of mourning in the treatment of the American and other dead in Iraq and in the controversy generated by the circulation of the photographs of the torture in Abu Ghraib prison. In the complex responses to these images I see small signs of hope for a recognition of the boundary problems not yet circumscribed by the traditional languages of outrage and defense. Then, in chapter 4, "Theory in the Time of Death," I seek to develop these possibilities by way of some of the insights of theory, that conventionally marginalized foreign body, for an understanding of the systematic *and* historical-empirical situation in which we find ourselves needing to know once again but perhaps for the first time after 9/11. The power of theory is often held to be that it does not obsess over empirical or particular details, aiming instead at some level of abstraction and systematic analysis; that power can only be enhanced when its findings are seen to be in line with so many of the empirical and particular events that have come into focus after and around 9/11. Rhetorically I must here take the risk of being seen to exploit 9/11 as an opportune occasion for a defense of theory. Substantially I hope to persuade any skeptical readers that theory is not the "other" that requires such a defense, but a genre of inquiry and explanation that we, given our relatively shrunken and increasingly shrinking lexical reserve, would be well advised to sustain. Those who do not need to be convinced of this will I hope still find some value in a demonstration of just how pertinent the power of theory is to an urgent world situation. The crazy foreign cousins whose languages we never quite deciphered, whose names are Baudrillard, Derrida, Žižek, and Agamben among others, have come back home and have something to say that is worth hearing.

The World Trade Towers never did fully belong to the world in their empirical life; it is our job to try to supplement that name and claim in their afterlife. Or, in the words of the most striking of all the commemorative messages I have seen or heard of painted on the walls and pillars around the World Trade Center site: "This is history—don't make it mystery."[18] Right next to it is another message: "To all who fought for our country: we will survive, always, God bless us forever." Then, elsewhere, there is another: "Kill all Muslims."[19] These three slogans embody ideology, its critique, and a vicious if predictable racism. They exist (or existed) among many

18. I have recently seen this phrase attributed to Harry Roland, an "unofficial greeter and guide" at the World Trade Center site. See Philip Noble, *Sixteen Acres: Architecture and the Outrageous Struggle for the Future of Ground Zero* (New York: Henry Holt, 2005), 232.

19. The first two I have seen myself; the third is cited in William Langeweische, "American Ground: Unbuilding the World Trade Center," *Atlantic Monthly*, July/August 2002, 50.

others, sitting side by side on concrete columns next to the World Trade Center site. The violence of the contradictions might disturb us but should also give us some hope for a less mystified future: there is a lot to be worked through. I end this book with a discussion of Muslims, though not the ones meant by the author of the third message. Even this language, believe it or not, is not devoid of a productive complexity.

1

Remembering the Dead

An Essay upon Epitaphs

PORTRAITS OF GRIEF

Among the many things that changed after September 11, 2001, was the policy on obituaries in the *New York Times*. For weeks after the attack on the World Trade Towers the newspaper printed fifteen or so brief remembrances a day of some of the almost three thousand people who died in the towers, in the airplanes, and during the rescue efforts. The leaders of corporations, entertainers, politicians, and other more or less public figures whose place in the world would have ordinarily assured them a place on the standard obituary page continued to appear there. The additional full pages of photographs and memorials were for the ordinary people, the firefighters, window washers, janitors, and waiters whose lives and deaths would normally have gone unrecorded by the most widely circulated newspaper in the United States, the newspaper of record for much of the nation. Here they were arrayed alongside the company executives and corporate leaders who also died on September 11; all were accorded the same size photograph and the same number of column inches. The *Times* was declaring itself at this most tragic time as a paper for all New Yorkers and all Americans and attempting to pay proper homage to the ubiquity of death and the mournful democracy of grief. A parallel series of memorials to those killed in the attack on the Pentagon also appeared in the same newspaper, part of the separate section devoted day after day to the events of September 11 and their ongoing consequences.

The "Portraits of Grief" were nationally syndicated, and readers across the country found these brief notices, with their blurred images of smiling, living people photographed at mostly happy moments, to be very moving and meaningful, powerfully evocative of what had happened and could never be forgotten. One wrote a letter suggesting that they should be made part of a formal memorial at the site of the World Trade Center. Another responded to their recording of a significant number of transnational and cross-racial couples and of functional families in which many of the parenting obligations were fulfilled by the men, seeing these as impressive paradigms of the new civil society: America works. The notices were not in fact straightforward obituaries, because they preserved a rather decorous ambiguity, a hope that some might still come out alive or be found wandering the streets of Manhattan; so they were called "glimpses of some of the victims" or "glimpses of some of those who have been declared dead." In the book that appeared in 2002 with a permanent record of the 1,910 portraits thus far published, they are called "snapshots of lives interrupted as they were being actively lived" or "anecdotes, tiny but telling details that seemed to reveal something true and essential about how each person lived."[1] As such they were intended as "concise, impressionistic, their power at least as much emotional as intellectual" (ix). They did not seek to present the sort of total summary of a life that would be expected of a traditional obituary. Above all they did not set out to decide on the worth of any of these lives in the recognized public sphere: "they were utterly democratic" (ix).

Democracy, in the words of Howell Raines, the chief editor, is above all beautiful and inspiring: "when I read them, I am filled with an awareness of the subtle nobility of everyday existence, of the ordered beauty of quotidian lives for millions of Americans, of the unforced dedication with which our fellow citizens go about their duties as parents, life partners, employers or employees, as planters of community gardens, coaches of the young, joyful explorers of this great land and the world beyond its shores" (vii). The record of tragically truncated mundane lives appearing day after day—this person enjoyed vaca-

---

1. *Portraits, 9/11/01: The Collected "Portraits of Grief" from the New York Times,* with a foreword by Howell Raines, introduction by Janny Scott (New York: Henry Holt/Times Books, 2002), vii, ix.

tions in Florida, that person loved her nieces and nephews, this person sent money home every week to South America, that person loved to cook—began to make us realize, day after day, and in a more than abstract way, just how many lives constitute approximately three thousand, and how indiscriminate death, all death, really is. The notices recalled the simple things in life, presumably the things that the bereaved wished to report about their loved ones. At first it seemed unlikely that everyone could be remembered in this way. But the notices kept coming, day after day, week after week. The sheer enormity of the effort to personalize this many deaths made us feel that everyone and everyman was here, or could be here. The names and faces and life stories were indeed those of ordinary people, not the notables who have traditionally provided the content of the obituary columns. And yet powerful as they were, read in batches of a few at a time, the collective impression of these snapshots was and is troubling. They were clearly being put to work in the cause of a patriotic momentum that Raines's words make very clear. None here cheated on her spouse or abused his children, or was indifferent to community activities. One tends of course to speak only good things of the dead, but even within the expected bounds of memorial decorum, the notices seem formulaic. They seem regimented, even militarized, made to march to the beat of a single drum. I will return to this.

But the notices are indeed democratic in the simplest and most minimal sense: everyone is there, or everyone whose nearest of kin wanted them to be there (many did refuse). The alphabetically organized book version of the "Portraits" includes in its first few entries the expected investment bankers and executives but also a cleaner, a restaurant worker, and a foreign tourist. Each snapshot is roughly the same length: there are no distinctions of class, income, or ethnicity. It was not always thus in times of suffering, terror, or war. In the distant past, when kings were kings and ordinary people held to be worthless or beneath acknowledgment, there was no effort to remember commoners. In a famous passage at the end of the fourth act of Shakespeare's *Henry V,* the young king asks his herald to report details of the English dead at Agincourt. The herald hands over a paper, and the king reads as follows:

Edward, the Duke of York, the Earl of Suffolk,
Sir Richard Ketly, Davy Gam, esquire;

None else of name; and of all other men
But five and twenty. (IV.viii. 105–8)

The French have lost 10,000, of whom all but 1,600 were persons of "blood and quality" (line 92). There is debate over the degree to which Shakespeare intends irony at the king's expense at this point in the cycle, but there is only a slim case to be made for Henry's being here exposed as an insensitive elitist (*esquire* of course takes its older sense and specifies a person of substance). Only four English notables have died, along with twenty-five others. They are not of name and so pass unnamed.

Starting sometime in the nineteenth century, the need to commemorate the deaths of ordinary people began to be felt in Britain. In the United States it seems to have been in place somewhat earlier. By 1918, as those brought up in British and American towns and villages know all too well, the scope of commemoration of the military dead had extended to all ranks, and all are named. Their names are legion—90 men (and boys) in my hometown in England, a town of no more than 3,000 or so in 1914. I used to think that this list must include the dead from the neighboring villages, which, perhaps, did not erect monuments of their own (since they were paid for largely by public subscription).[2] But four miles up the road, the next village has its own war memorial, its own list of 43 dead in the Great War of 1914–18. A total of 54 "boys" from my old school, a small country grammar school, "gave" their lives in the two wars. Eleven thousand Norfolk men and boys, 2.5 percent of the population of the county, died in the Great War alone. The figures are numbing, and they remain so as one moves to the larger towns and cities. York Minster commemorates the deaths of 8,814 men of the York and Lancaster Regiment and the more than 9,400 of the Yorkshire Light Infantry who fell in the First World War.

In Britain it is in the nineteenth-century memorials in the great cathedrals that one can begin to plot the passages of those of "no name" taking on names. York Minster records all names and ranks

---

2. The Imperial War Graves Commission apparently spent about £8 million on British cemeteries in France—the equivalent of about two days' worth of ammunition expended at the battle of Passchendaele; see Reinhart Koselleck, *The Practice of Conceptual History: Timing History, Spacing Concepts,* trans. Todd Samuel Presner, Kerstin Behnke, and Jobst Welge (Stanford: Stanford University Press, 1992), 359.

of the regimental dead in the South Africa War (1899–1902). So it does for the dead in the Russian War (1854–55), the 42 who died in the Sudan (1884–87), and the 40 who perished in the New Zealand Wars (1845–66), though here only death in combat merits a name; there are "also 126 from other causes." The Indian Wars of 1871–84 list only 9 officers by name, but the 18 men who died at sea in June 1854, aboard what I assume was a naval transport ship, are all named in a monument erected in 1858. The earliest monument naming all ranks is that put in place in 1855 to the dead of the Burma War of 1852–53. There is a memorial to those who died in the "Wars of 1808–15," which lists 40 or so officers of the King's Own Yorkshire Light Infantry by name and goes on to mention that 610 men of other ranks are commemorated on a scroll in the depository. But it turns out that the memorial tablet itself dates from 1913, which perhaps explains its punctilious reference to the ordinary deaths recorded in the archive.[3] These records are indeed derived from regimental lists kept at the time of the Napoleonic Wars, which must have been in response to a directive apparently issued by the Duke of York to his commanders in 1797, the first of its kind, to report all of the war dead by name.[4] But no formal or bureaucratic mechanisms seem to have existed for getting that information back to the families of the dead. And because the French wars evolved into battles between huge fleets and enormous armies, with massive casualties, that would not have been easy. De Quincey's anecdote of riding with the mail into "some little town" after the battle of Talavera in July 1809 makes the point. When he meets the anxious mother of a soldier in a regiment he knows from his newspaper to have been decimated in the battle—only one in four surviving—he does not have a list of the names of the dead.[5] At Waterloo in 1815 there were approximately 70,000 in each of the French and allied armies facing one another; thousands died in a day.

3. After my own walk around the York Minster, reported in David Simpson, "Naming the Dead," *London Review of Books*, November 15, 2001, 3–7, my colleague Catherine Robson checked with Jeremy Muldowney on site, who revealed the late date of this memorial plaque. My thanks to both.

4. Clive Emsley, *British Society and the French Wars, 1793–1815* (London: Macmillan, 1979), 93.

5. *The Collected Works of Thomas De Quincey*, 14 vols., ed. David Masson (Edinburgh: Adam and Charles Black, 1890), 13:299.

The hero of Waterloo, the Duke of Wellington, has been many times remembered for apparently referring to his soldiers as the scum of the earth, not a sentiment that seems to be indicative of any newly discovered respect for the lives and deaths of ordinary people. Nonetheless, Lukács has argued that the European wars of the Napoleonic period were indeed the first to involve citizen armies on such a grand scale, and that this circumstance was responsible for the development of a national consciousness and a "mass experience" among those formerly deemed not worth naming, the rank and file.[6] This seems to have taken some time to become translated into funereal ritual. The process of cultivating respect for the corpses of ordinary people, and the habit of recording their names in public places, seems to have been at best uneven. Here is an entry from the *London Observer* of November 18, 1822:

WAR AND COMMERCE.—It is estimated that more than a million of bushels of human and inhuman bones were imported last year from the continent of Europe into the port of Hull. The neighborhood of Leipzic, Austerlitz, Waterloo, and of all of the places where, during the late bloody war, the principal battles were fought, have been swept alike of the bones of the hero and of the horse which he rode. Thus collected from every quarter, they have been shipped to the port of Hull, and thence forwarded to the Yorkshire bone-grinders, who have erected steam-engines and powerful machinery, for the purpose of reducing them to a granulary state. In this condition they are sent chiefly to Doncaster, one of the largest agricultural markets in that part of the country, and are there sold to the farmers to manure their lands. The oily substance gradually evolving as the base calcines, makes a more substantial manure than any other substance, particularly human bones. It is now ascertained beyond a doubt, by actual experiment on an extensive scale, that a dead soldier is a most valuable article of commerce; and, for ought known to the contrary, the good farmers of Yorkshire are, in a great measure, indebted to the bones of their children for their daily bread. It is certainly a singular fact, that Great Britain should have sent out such multitudes of soldiers to

6. Georg Lukács, *The Historical Novel*, trans. Hannah Mitchell and Stanley Mitchell (Lincoln: University of Nebraska Press, 1983), 23.

fight the battles of this country upon the continent of Europe, and should then import their bones as an article of commerce to fatten her soil![7]

The passage is mind-boggling—so much so that we are bound to be radically doubtful. Perhaps this is some Swiftian satire on the insensitivity of the modern agricultural economy? A piece of journalistic invention, quietly inserted into the "Miscellaneous, Chiefly Domestic" column and designed to embarrass the nation into doing something about the bodies buried on the battlefield? Or perhaps it is an accurate record? Already we seem to be in the unsettling world of virtuality that so preoccupies our contemporary theorists of the postmodern, a world in which nothing can be assumed to be what it seems—video, photograph, eyewitness account—and in which everything can be called into doubt as mere propaganda by those who have an interest in so doing. Poets such as Byron made much of the fertilizing functions of the Waterloo dead, and elegists such as Tennyson have taken comfort in the appearance of spring flowers over graves.[8] But bone grinders? Manure? Big business? There is nothing in subsequent editions of the *Observer* for 1822 to give us a sure sign of how we are to read this passage: no follow-up. If a true account, this train of events suggests that in 1822 Britain still had some way to go before the sanctity of battlefields and places of mass annihilation was established. Presumably the notable dead had by then been removed from the earth on which they fell and properly buried in Brussels, or in their local churches and country houses. But who knows if an officer or two might not have been lying with his men? Where man and horse are ground together, it seems absurdly fastidious to inquire into the differences between the ranks. Writing in 1845 under the pseudonym of Michael Angelo Titmarsh, Thackeray protested the indifference to ordinary men in the commemoration culture after Waterloo:

7. *Observer,* November 18, 1822. Samuel Hynes cites part of this passage in *The Soldiers' Tale: Bearing Witness to Modern War* (New York: Viking, 1997), 17, and it has been reproduced by others using Hynes's text as the source.

8. Koselleck, *Practice of Conceptual History,* 320, cites a plan for a French Revolutionary cemetery that would have used the bones of the dead as building materials so that "the dead would be identical with their commemorative memorial."

I felt very much disappointed at not seeing the names of the *men* as well as the officers. Are they to be counted for nought? A few more inches of marble to each monument would have given space for all the names of the men; and the men of that day were the winners of the battle. We have a right to be as grateful individually to any given private as to any given officer; their duties were very much the same. Why should the country reserve its gratitude for the genteel occupiers of the army-list, and forget the gallant fellows whose humble names were written in the regimental books?[9]

Waterloo was a tourist attraction even while the battle was going on, as the fashionable and curious rode out from Brussels to watch the events unfold. Human remains were not uncommonly among their souvenirs.[10]

Contrast Lower Manhattan in the days and weeks after 9/11, when tourists were strictly forbidden, curious onlookers sent packing, and even journalists and professional photographers pushed away by angry firemen and other workers with the declaration that they were trespassing on "sacred ground." Human relics, even the tiniest fragments of human bodies, were painstakingly excavated from the enormous piles of rubble, carefully documented, and put through DNA testing in hopes of being able to send something, however small, to the families of the dead for conventional burial. One family received no fewer than three separate shipments of body parts, each of which was duly interred at a funeral service. Among the reasons for the unarguably futile outpouring of donated blood from the general population (responding to a Red Cross appeal) must surely have been a fantasy that somehow there would be survivors, and that those survivors would be repairable, merely wounded, whole enough in body to be topped up and sent on their way. It was not so. Little remained, so that bodies and body parts became absolutely precious and were accorded unprecedented levels of respect and attention. There were no bone merchants lining

9. William Makepeace Thackeray [Michelangelo Titmarsh], "Little Sketches and Road-Side Travels: Waterloo: No. III," *Fraser's Magazine for Town and Country* 31 (1845): 95. My thanks to Catherine Robson for bringing this to my attention.

10. See Philip Shaw, *Waterloo and the Romantic Imagination* (Basingstoke, UK: Palgrave Macmillan, 2002), 67.

up their carts—there would have been little for them to have collected if there had been.

This radical contrast in the treatment of the British dead in 1822—if the story is true—and the civilian dead of 2001 reminds us forcefully, if we need reminding, that death is a cultural event as well as an inevitable fate for us all. The history of the dead in the United States reveals a very different profile from that evidenced in nineteenth-century Britain. The events of April 19, 1775, at Lexington and Concord were from the first commemorated as instances of the dignity and importance of ordinary lives. Those who died on the American side were after all militiamen, citizen volunteers, rather than conventionally enlisted soldiers, and their numbers were relatively few, making it possible to celebrate their courage as individuals. By 1799 a monument was erected naming the eight who had died on Lexington Green and who had become exemplary not just of a national liberation movement but of a divine purpose. By 1829 Ezra Ripley could pronounce the Concord Old North Bridge as "little less than holy, and really consecrated by Heaven to the cause of liberty and the Rights of man."[11] We are well on the way to the nomination of part of Lower Manhattan as sacred ground. The commemoration of Lexington and Concord established some important and recurring precedents: the dead were neither purely soldiers nor civilians, but both at once, and we can see the traces of this syndrome in the memorializing of the civilian dead of 9/11. The militiamen were few and ordinary, not nobles, and their sacrifice was sanctified by appeals to Divine Providence as itself the engine of the national destiny. So too the dead of 9/11 have been made to figure in grander narratives of national futures and civic virtues than any of them could probably have imagined or perhaps desired.

The celebration of individual sacrifices was not apparently replicated in those theaters of the Revolutionary War in which casualties were greater and the pressure of time and numbers more compelling: Valley Forge, where more than 3,000 Americans died, has only one marked grave.[12] So too the early battles of the Civil War

11. I owe this account to Edward Tabor Linenthal, *Sacred Ground: Americans and Their Battlefields*, 2nd ed. (Urbana: University of Illinois Press, 1993), 13–29.

12. See Kristin Ann Hass, *Carried to the Wall: American Memory and the Vietnam Veterans Memorial* (Berkeley and Los Angeles: University of California Press, 1998), 43.

gave rise to mass burials in unmarked graves. But the providential narrative reappears at Gettysburg, the turning point of the campaign and the sign, perhaps, that at least on the Union side the rank and file were enlisting in a cause held to be as much divine as secular, and their sacrifice thus far more than merely dutiful or political. Union followers were prompt in picking out the bodies of their own troops on the field of Gettysburg, already described in Lincoln's famous address of November 19, 1863, as beyond further consecration or hallowing because of the primary sacrifice itself.[13] The story of the events surrounding the new burial culture established at Gettysburg is a complex one, and Kristin Hass gives a helpful abbreviated version: two rival local lawyers seeking to make reputations, one of whom, David McConaughy, uses the term "sacred ground" in 1863; the need to lift the morale of an army no longer made up of volunteers but now raised by conscription; and the response to federal and state legislation about the treatment of the dead.[14] The buy-out policy still ensured that a large percentage of fighting troops came from the poor and immigrant classes, as they apparently had during the Revolutionary War—not everyone who fell in battle was a typical Concord or Lexington minuteman. But this practice became harder to sustain or justify as the casualties mounted, and some attention to the bodies and the memory of the dead must have been intended partly to soften the discontent. Already by 1863 and 1864, memorials naming the dead were appearing in northern towns and villages—a number of which would claim to be first in the nation to so honor its soldiers. At least one critic has seen in the sanctification of violent death in the Civil War the origins of an ongoing tradition whereby "aggression is the condition of national belonging" and rendered so by a "state-sponsored culture struggling to invest dead bodies with common meaning."[15]

In the light of this complex historical situation—then and now—it is worth dwelling for a moment on Lincoln's use of the terms *hallow* and *hallowed*. The received sense of these words in this context would have us understand them as analogous to *sanctify* and *holy* or *sacred*, respectively. But there is a second meaning that runs along-

13. Linenthal, *Sacred Ground*, 89–93.

14. Hass, *Carried to the Wall*, 43–53.

15. Franny Nudelman, *John Brown's Body: Slavery, Violence, and the Culture of War* (Chapel Hill: University of North Carolina Press, 2004), 2, 78.

side the first: to *call* or *summon, to shout* or *cry out*. Both senses are embraced in the idea of actively consecrating, of *making* a place or thing sacred. It is thus striking that Lincoln so famously says that he cannot do this, that the site is already hallowed, that he is simply reporting what has already been achieved by the blood of the dead soldiers. But of course his address *is* doing just that: it is calling out and denominating, as only speech can do, a place that is otherwise yet open to definition, notwithstanding the blood in the soil. It is after all the address that does the hallowing—exactly what it denies by invoking a prior presence. All verbal commemorations and material monuments work in this way. They put in place what they claim is already there, and in so doing preempt the possibilities for alternative acts of memory. This is one reason why the design of monuments is so keenly contested.

The deaths of 9/11 thus occurred within a culture of commemoration that was already primed to resort to sanctification and personalization in the cause of upholding the image of a flourishing civil society and a providential national destiny, and one that inadvertently signals, as the Gettysburg Address signals, that it is doing exactly that. The pattern is not absolutely consistent—it seems to have taken some time, for example, to assemble the Alamo memorial and the myth of the Alamo.[16] But Lexington and Concord and Gettysburg are powerful precursors of the commemoration of 9/11. Since the Civil War we have often been collectively preoccupied with the dismal record of human cruelty and destructiveness typified above all, since the 1970s, by the all-encompassing image of the Holocaust. To be fully postmodern may indeed be to know that one lives without a full knowledge of history, and to worry about it; it definitely has seemed to involve being obsessed with memory and the memorial instinct. No single explanation can account for this. One thinks of the increased life expectancy and well-being experienced in the affluent parts of the world, which make death seem like the rude interruption of a good life rather than a necessary and ever-present force; of the dismal record of the last century and its genocides; and of course of the persuasions of the culture industry itself, which is headquartered in the anglophone first world and speaks to its anxieties and obsessions. Death

16. See Linenthal, *Sacred Ground*, 53–88.

is not only biological and personal, but also cultural, and more cultural than ever in a world in which the technologies of culture can reach so many—9/11 truly was a world event, witnessed in real or near-real time all across the world. The dead look different at different times and in different places. Acts of commemoration are staged for us and among us in the big-budget spectacle of the Hollywood movie: *Schindler's List, Titanic,* and *Saving Private Ryan* are the exemplary cases immediately preceding the event called 9/11. Much of recent "serious" fiction is about the past, about the ethics of remembrance, about deaths unatoned for. It is memorial fiction: think of *The English Patient, Time's Arrow, Cold Mountain, Atonement, The Remains of the Day,* the *Regeneration* trilogy, *Last Orders, Austerlitz, The Dream of Scipio,* and numerous others—a list which of course overlaps with that of the movie industry in more than a few cases. In the sphere of the visual arts, the curators of the Tate Modern in London have decided on the conjunction of History/Memory/Society as one of the sets of cognates goading school parties and otherwise open-minded visitors into meaningful associations: it is as if society exists by way of history and memory. Pierre Nora, as I have mentioned, performed a similar task for France. Germany has had its own intensified version of encounters with its past, typified by a simultaneous avowal of memory fatigue and an orgy of controversial memorialization in architecture, literature. and the arts.[17] In the more restricted sphere of the anglophone academy, the most widely circulated indicator of the New Historicism movement that overtook literary and cultural studies in the 1980s and 1990s was Stephen Greenblatt's anecdote about speaking with the dead: a phrase so potent in its summary of the Zeitgeist that its possible origin in a purely literary rather than (or as well as) experiential archive—Eliot's *The Waste Land*—has passed almost without notice.

Military deaths, or so it would seem from my less than exhaustive survey, have been recorded more or less democratically since the middle of the nineteenth century; everyone who dies in combat is recorded, or is likely to be recorded. Perhaps the Great War did

17. A fine account of this can be found in Andreas Huyssen, *Twilight Memories: Marking Time in a Culture of Amnesia* (New York and London: Routledge, 1995); and idem, *Present Pasts: Urban Palimpsests and the Politics of Memory* (Stanford: Stanford University Press, 2003).

not so much in this respect create modern memory, as Paul Fussell's magisterial *The Great War and Modern Memory* has argued that it did, as bring to the fore what had emerged in the "smaller" wars of the previous century, and in the very large war in America: those who died fighting for their country deserved being named and remembered by name.[18] The dead of the American Civil War were accorded the dignity of dying either in a holy cause (on the Union side) or in defense of home, family, and locality (the Confederate alternative). Of course in the nineteenth-century British case it seldom was a matter of dying for one's country, any more than it would be in 1914. Historians have found it notoriously difficult to justify why anyone should have died in the Great War, or to specify convincingly why it had to happen and what benefits were achieved by such an appalling sacrifice of lives. Presumably the organizers and publicists of the smaller wars of Victoria's reign felt that naming the dead, all the dead, was the least they could do to compensate those mothers and fathers who lost their children for a place or territory they themselves would never see and did not care about. England's dead, as Felicia Hemans's poem on that topic presciently tells us, are all over the place, in the oceans, deserts, and polar wastes, not always properly buried, and often in bits and pieces. In the face of such indignity, a name on a monument might have seemed but a small consolation, though perhaps some were thus consoled. A local habitation is devised and a name is written in stone out of the imagined corner of a foreign field and the expenditure of life. During the Great War the lists of the unrecovered dead, those "missing presumed dead," reached almost unimaginable figures. In the summer of 1916 some 72,000 of the German casualties were accounted for, while 86,000 were missing or mutilated beyond recognition.[19] On the British and allied side the memorials at the Menin Gate, Neuve Chapelle, and of course Thiepval and

18. Jay Winter, *Sites of Memory, Sites of Mourning: The Great War in European Cultural History* (Cambridge: Cambridge University Press, 1995), 3, 5, 76, has disputed Fussell's assumptions about the Great War as the origin of a new cultural order. Thomas W. Laqueur, "Memory and Naming in the Great War," in *Commemorations: The Politics of National Identity*, ed. John R. Gillis (Princeton: Princeton University Press, 1994), 151–67, notes that only in 1916 were the bodies of the British dead gathered up for internment in marked graves (153).

19. Koselleck, *Practice of Conceptual History*, 319.

various other places were covered with thousands of names to which no bodies could be attached.[20]

Those who died on September 11, 2001, were civilians, but civilians who could be and were readily identified with a national cause, victims of an attack on America and on democracy itself, the very medium of the dignity of ordinary life. In its reports on the sinking of the *Titanic* in April 1912, the *New York Times* had grappled once before with the task of recording the deaths of ordinary people, those not of name who drowned along with the rich and famous. A sense of this can be had from perusing the facsimile pages of the special commemorative edition put out by the same newspaper on April 15, 1998, to respond to the runaway box-office success of James Cameron's film. The large-print captions are devoted to the "notable passengers" and "noted men" on board the ship, and there are extended quasi-obituaries of many of them. But the *Times* also makes an effort to record the names of all the missing and all the survivors, including the third-class steerage passengers, and to tabulate the exact numbers of each, in figures that changed from day to day as new information came in. The third-class dead are named, but there are no obituaries. By way of contrast the London *Times*, faced with reporting on the bombing in late 1940 (the Blitz), does not give the names of the huge number of civilian casualties. It seems to have had a strict policy of naming only the military victims. The Roll of Honour contains all names of all ranks of persons who died or were missing in action in all of the services, including the merchant marine, and extending to the crews of trawlers enlisted as minesweepers. Officers make it onto the formal obituary page, sometimes with an appended "personal tribute" that makes familiar sense of their lives: one man, besides being an officer, was a fine mechanic, loved sailing, and was clever at drawing and sketching. And those whose families presumably felt that they were of importance are listed on the front page under the categories "On Active Service" and "Missing." A.R.P. (Air Raid Precautions) wardens who died in the air raids are named, perhaps because they are more or less military personnel. And one couple who made a miraculous escape are given names in the issue of November 11, 1940: Mr. and

---

20. Laqueur, "Memory and Naming," 153–55; see also Winter, *Sites of Memory*, 39–44.

Mrs. A. H. Button. Otherwise, the ordinary dead are not mentioned by name. They are, however, at times movingly personalized. Here is one paragraph from the *Times*, November 12, 1940:

> Six members of one family, including a three-week-old baby, were killed when a high-explosive bomb demolished a house in the London area. The family were celebrating the christening of the baby, and its christening cake was afterwards found among the wreckage. The killed were a retired police sergeant who had returned to police duties at the outbreak of war, his wife and her mother, their daughter and her husband and child. An unmarried daughter was the only survivor. (2)

To be sure, events were unfolding at such a pace in so many places and with such scarce resources that the gathering of personal data about the ordinary dead would have been a gargantuan task. But one still gets the sense of a different culture at work here. Churchill's war cabinet and its media outlets were by no means immune to the appeal of good propaganda, as the pages of photographs of getting in the harvest all over England in the autumn of 1940 make perfectly clear. But for some reason there is no urge to represent the lives and faces of the dead, or even to name them. It is hard to decide among cynical prudence, class-ridden prejudice, or honest delicacy as the motive for this. The pathos of the dead family is real, but different from that operative in post–9/11 issues of the *New York Times*. We are not told their names; we do not hear about their virtues as citizens and parents. Here there seems to have been no obvious and compelling urge to record the identities and past lives of the beloved dead. Perhaps Churchill imagined only negative publicity from an extensive and ongoing naming of the civilian dead at a time when the war was not going well for Britain. Perhaps the editors at the London *Times* saw little of importance in the lives of ordinary people. Perhaps grief was held to be properly private and not to be published for all to read about. It is not impossible that something of all of these motivations might have been at work.

William Wordsworth thought about memorial practices in his three "Essays upon Epitaphs" published between 1810 and 1812 at a time when England's dead had for some years been accumulating in various places on the earth. Wordsworth does not engage with the military deaths of his own generation, though we can assume that these must have been on the minds of everyone; he writes instead about the epitaphic tradition in general, and particularly as it is evident in English churchyards, as if the whole matter of wasted life and unrecovered or dismembered or hopelessly distant bodies could be gathered within a domestic and familiar trope, the green spot in the green shade. Wordsworth notes that the epitaph tends to record the good in everyone, as if they had lived in a world without cruelty or evil or mere human failings: "the affections are their own justification" and give rise to "truth hallowed by love— the joint offspring of the worth of the dead and the affections of the living."[21] So too the *New York Times* gave us a world in which every one of the victims was engaged in some visibly good life: taking care of others, bringing joy, lovingly looking after children. It is the given truth of democratic culture that, in Wordsworth's words, "every man has a character of his own, to the eye that has skill to perceive it" (56). It may also be the case that the approved rhetoric for describing those lives depends on not looking too closely and that attention to individual character is not the primary purpose of . public commemoration.

DISHONORING THE DEAD?

Homage to what Wordsworth calls "character" is indeed not quite what we find in the "glimpses of the victims" of September 11. Notwithstanding their individualized profiles, they all seem to have lived virtuous lives as loving parents, spouses, siblings, and pillars of their communities. Reading the profiles in sequence, we find that they all start to sound the same, with only minute variations on the governing themes. The array of difference and creative idiosyncrasy that is often described as the proper core of a liberal democracy is here oddly flattened out, or expended on hobbies and leisure time. Most of all, hardly any of them are described as if their jobs and careers were stressful, and many are remembered in terms that barely mention what they did. The collective effort works toward the representation of a common humanity and inevitably plays

21. *The Prose Works of William Wordsworth*, 3 vols., ed. W. J. B. Owen and Jane Worthington Smyser (Oxford: Clarendon Press, 1974), 2:57–58.

down the degree to which the World Trade Center was a complex subculture running according to a highly divided system of labor with massively discrepant rewards. The format of the photographs and the short biographies appended to them almost inevitably recalls the genre of the high school year book, the register of lives only just about to be launched into the world of complex responsibility, for the most part not yet marked by accumulated disappointment or distress. Many of the portraits tell of immigrants who were working hard for a better life and believed that they had found it. (Those from Muslim cultures are only infrequently identified as religious.) We read of the man who loved his pet fish, and talked to them, but learn nothing about his job. And when a person's job was that of an investment banker, we hear mostly about how much he loved to sail. So too there is the firefighter who loved to cook, the claims adjustor who fed stray cats, the man who kissed his sleeping children every night before he went to bed.

[Can we think and talk about these matters in this way without appearing to dishonor the dead? Can we be moved by these stories, as millions of readers were, and still entertain anything of a critical perspective? On both counts I think we can; I think we must. The dead of 9/11 undoubtedly had a good deal more "character" than the formulaic or prudent celebrations of the published portraits were recording. One might say, with Wordsworth, that the brief memorial is not the place for recording quirks and rough edges, the frustrations we all feel and the failings we all possess. True enough. But the nature and form of the leveling out is not just a matter of memorial decorum: there is a genre being deployed here, and an editorial in the New York Times—another brief essay on epitaphs— more or less admitted it. The author tells us that "each profile is only a snapshot, a single still frame lifted from the unrecountable complexity of a lived life," and admits, albeit unwittingly, that there is a pattern: "We recognize the archetypes that define the ways these stories are told. The tales of courtship and aspiration, the ways these people relaxed and how they related to their children— these are really our own stories, translated into a slightly different, next-door key."[22] The word "archetypes" is loaded: it suggests that we are in the presence of eternally recurring human motives or

22. "Among the Missing," New York Times, October 14, 2001, WK12.

qualities, so that the phrase "our own stories" comes to designate not the rather specific desires of a group of actual or aspiring middle-class Americans, or perhaps just the manufactured image of what that specific group should desire) but the narratives of a universal human instinct. The author becomes even more transparently ideological as we are told that "nearly everyone who died in the towers that day was either living in the midst of an achieved ambition or had set out on the way to achieving it," so that "these profiles also offer a map of fulfillment." The ambition of the man who washed the windows might have been rather different from that of the person about to make partner in a law firm or investment corporation, but that question is never raised, indeed it is aggressively displaced. The same editorial goes on to say that "the generosity, the selflessness, that emanates from these stories is remarkable." Getting, spending, fulfilling ambitions or simply making it through the day are not, it is to be made clear, at odds with the most lavish habits of doing good to others. The snapshot obituaries are being put to work to counter the much-publicized decline of civil society that has made a best seller out of, for example, Robert Putnam's *Bowling Alone*. They are telling us, at this moment of extreme vulnerability, that corporate America (or international finance) in partnership with infinite reserves of personal charity were creating a wonderful life that has now so tragically been destroyed for so many.

Furthermore, these obituaries were not the spontaneous outpouring of unassisted natural feelings. They were assembled and significantly composed by a team of editors at the *Times* who worked with the bereaved relatives to produce them: a few families refused; others refused and changed their minds later. The obituaries were syndicated across the country and reprinted, as I have mentioned, as a hardback volume available through the office of the newspaper. This was never the realm of pure reportage, the uninflected passing on of preexisting information. Howell Raines, the editor who subsequently was obliged to resign after he was revealed as responsible for failing to check the sources of a reporter found to have filed fake stories on other topics, is more than a little embarrassing in his joyous recollections of the aesthetic and professional satisfactions of the first days after 9/11:

The papers we produced were hailed for their visual power, but it was the written content that accounted for the extent of our

Pulitzer sweep. While going at a dead run to cover the fast-breaking news of the post–9/11 period, Jon Landman and a group of his editors and reporters invented the "Portraits of Grief" series. Those thumbnail sketches of every person who has died in the World Trade Center disaster became, in effect, a national shrine, and were a strong ingredient of the special daily section "A Nation Challenged," which we published for the last quarter of 2001. That special section helped the *Times* win the Pulitzer Board's highest honor: the award for public service.[23]

It might seem churlish to seek to deprive Mr. Raines of his remembered moment in the sun as he is looking back on a foreshortened career, but his urge to make such self-congratulatory virtue out of these dark events should not pass without comment. The journalistic credit extended to those who "invented" the "Portraits of Grief" lets slip the degree to which they really *were* invented, just as the much-coveted public service award suggests recognition of the ideological effort contained in the portraits as a legitimation of the American way of life: an instance of verbal flag-waving. Raines continues his narrative:

> I've never worked with greater pride or been more eager to get to the office each day than in those frantic months between 9/11 and the end of the Afghan war. . . . In putting out "A Nation Challenged" we sometimes gathered as many as twenty-five people—not just text editors but also designers and artists, layout and photo editors, long treated as second-class citizens—around the big table where we selected and organized stories and photographs. . . . Nothing that has happened since can dim the luster of those memories. I wouldn't trade those first six months for another decade as executive editor.

Again the assumptions and conclusions are telling, even if we do not dispute the notion that the Afghan war has ended. The self-approving dissolution of class boundaries between editors and lesser workers around the big table is a visible facsimile of the same task of creating the common man that the snapshots themselves were performing. The event of 9/11 was, it seems, like the sinking

23. Howell Raines, "My Times," *Atlantic Monthly*, May 2004, 68.

of the *Titanic:* good news for the image of the democracy, not just at the national ideological level but in the smaller workplace of the newspaper of record.

The patriotic effort thus merges into and emerges out of a commercial one: the two are not simply distinguishable. Neither is simply the cause of the other, but without both we wonder whether either would have been open to this kind of articulation and circulation. The professional development of the executive editor of the *New York Times* is not incompatible with the remembering of the dead; instrumentally, each facilitates the other. Fast forward to the spring of 2004, however, by way of another war, and we see a different story: the much-discussed apology that the *Times* felt it had to print (inside pages, no pictures, no Pulitzer awards) in order to respond to the growing volume of criticism of its pusillanimous and perhaps knowingly dishonest reporting of the events leading to— and justifying—the Iraq war. The moment of hyperbolic pride and the moment of shame are connected. The representation of the almost 3,000 dead as an icon of America and of the Twin Towers as a synecdoche for the nation surely contributed to a largely uncritical application of the language of war (as if between nation states) and thus to the uncritical linkage of bin Laden's nonnational terrorist movement with Saddam Hussein's otherwise unimplicated Iraq. And from there the creation of even more dead—so far (as of June 2005) over 1,700 Americans and many, many thousands of uncounted Iraqis. The *New York Times* these days prints the names of the American dead in small corners of the inside pages: no "Portraits of Grief" for them. Of the Iraqi dead, who might according to the figures reported by *Lancet* have numbered over 100,000 by 2004, there is little or no word.

As I have said, the "Portraits of Grief" were not epitaphs but "snapshots" that became, with the passing of time and the knowledge that those missing would not turn up, unofficial obituaries. The epitaph, as Wordsworth knew well, takes its credibility from being in close proximity to the remains of the dead person it recalls. As such it "feeds also local attachment, which is the tap-root of the tree of Patriotism."[24] But the "glimpses of the victims" of September 11 could not exist in any physical proximity to the

24. Wordsworth, *Prose Works*, 2:93.

remains of the dead. They functioned in a purely associative and virtual sense; the victims died in New York, and this was the *New York Times*. They fed national attachment as they were circulated across the country in local newspapers—a virtual memorial in daily installments. Those few among the bereaved who did receive a conventional body for burial were able to go through the traditional rituals whose roles are complex but familiar. Robert Pogue Harrison claims with some conviction that "to be human means above all to bury."[25] Weaving Vico and Heidegger into a powerful argument for the fundamental importance of burying, preserving, and continually acknowledging the dead to any sustainable model of human identity and human habitation, Harrison indirectly illuminates all the elements of traditional memorial culture that are confounded and withheld by the conditions of 9/11.[26] If houses and palaces were founded on the graves of our ancestors, reminding us (as does the imagined experience of the returning and unappeased dead) that our very being is a being toward death, and civilization itself—house and home—a memorial to our forefathers and an effort to live up to their example, then the abrogation of foundational associations must be one among the threats that 9/11 embodies. This was, however, hardly new: it reflects elements of the modern world that Heideggerian localism, of the sort that Harrison restates, was devised to counter or critique. It has been both the condition of empire, with its dissemination of bodies across the world and its oceans, and the result of modern warfare's investment in high explosives, from the cannons of Waterloo and Gettysburg to the atomic bomb and its "smart" successors. It has also been a feature of modern genocide. To stand before the lists of names that make up such memorials as Thiepval and the Vietnam Wall (in the case of the genocides there have been too many names to list in this way) is to realize that they are just that, names cut in stone, detached from any of the comforts that accrue from taking

25. Robert Pogue Harrison, *The Dominion of the Dead* (Chicago: University of Chicago Press, 2003), xi.

26. Derrida makes a similar point in claiming that "there is no culture without a culture of death" and in conflating hospitality with the "abode as last resting place," presupposing "waiting, the horizon of waiting and the preparation of welcoming [acceuil]: *from life to death*." See Jacques Derrida, *Acts of Religion*, ed. Gil Anidjar (New York and London: Routledge, 2002), 361.

the dead into the earth, standing beside their graves, or scattering their ashes.[27] Some are indeed buried elsewhere, but many are not—the bodies never recovered, or buried where they died, or blown or burned into so many fragments that no body existed at all. The power of the various tombs of unknown soldiers derives from their standing in the place of the bodies that never came home, or found home. The event called 9/11 was for many of the dead another case of the total destruction of the body, and thus it threatens what Harrison calls "the free retrieval and renewal of legacy."[28] Many of the victims did not have enough body left even to be imagined as haunting us, coming back in ghostly form: they passed straight from corporeal integrity to dust and vapor.[29] In the aftermath of the disaster, the NYPD made an effort to gather up handfuls of dust from the site, which were placed in urns and presented to the bereaved. Some of them surely contained some of the remains of some of the dead, but no one could tell to whom they belonged. So the rhetoric of the "Portraits of Grief," with its stress on family values, communitarian virtue, and seemingly adequate leisure amid busy lives (time for cooking, loving one's children, traveling, helping others) is detached not only from the fuller lives and "characters" of the dead themselves (the lives in which they might have been bad tempered or hated their jobs) but in most cases also from their physical remains. They are all that remains in the public record. The verbal fabric of consolation seems all the more incomplete—snapshot as obituary—given the common absence of a conventional grave site for the provision of alternative and repeatable solace.

The "Portraits of Grief" mostly resort to and reproduce a comforting sector of our verbal-ideological imaginary as their mode of response to death. Once in a while one reads a different story, a tale

27. The tomb of the Civil War unknowns, in which were gathered together unidentified body parts from the sequence of battles between Bull Run and the Rappahannock, was dedicated at Arlington National Cemetery in September 1866. A second Tomb of the Unknowns contains bodies representing the major foreign wars of the twentieth century. See www.arlingtoncemetery.com/contents.htm.

28. Harrison, *Dominion of the Dead,* 112.

29. Although Winter, *Sites of Memory,* 54–77, notes that there was an outpouring of spiritualism and of speaking with the dead in the wake of the Great War, from which so many bodies were not recovered.

of children whose grief cannot be appeased or of families having no consoling memories, and here one can sense the bleakness of bereaved existences that are not yet and may never be gathered up into patriotic success stories. But the majority of remembrances are defiantly positive, reports of the good times in these vanished lives. *Portraits* has entered popular culture as a patriotic icon. The response to 9/11 has also made significant marks on the common language. Notice the immediacy with which the media described and defined the site of the former World Trade Center as Ground Zero. This is technically correct in that the phrase is used to describe the place beneath and around an exploding bomb, and the fuel-filled jet planes were that, albeit in an unfamiliar form. The same phrase had appeared, oddly, in the reporting of the first World Trade Center bombing in 1993, from the pen of a journalist covering the event.[30] But the most habitual use of the term, as the *Oxford English Dictionary* tells us, is to designate an atomic explosion: the Trinity site in New Mexico, Hiroshima and Nagasaki, various sites in the Australian desert (hence it is the title of the 1988 film by Michael Pattinson and Bruce Myles), in Nevada or Siberia, in the Gobi Desert, in the South Pacific. The terrorist attack is thus assimilated to the many instances of nuclear explosions. But these have so far all been caused by nation-states and many caused by "us" and people on "our" side. One can see the connection of the 2001 event with the dropping of the bomb: there too, in Hiroshima and Nagasaki, hardly any bodies or body parts remained. There too most of the victims who died on those days were vaporized. There too no one had a clue what was coming out of a clear summer sky. But despite the physical analogy, the implications of other kinds of equivalences are dubious (and to say so is not at all to diminish the scope of the 9/11 tragedy but merely to question the uses to which it is being put.)

The implicit declaration of moral equivalence is especially troubling. On the one hand, it could be said that this event places the United States fully and for the first time within the tragical

---

30. Cited in Robert S. Nelson and Margaret Olin, eds., *Monuments and Memory, Made and Unmade* (Chicago: University of Chicago Press, 2003), 311. It also figured in the reporting of the first Gulf War as the site of U.S. aggression, e.g., Robert Wiener, *Live from Baghdad: Gathering News at Ground Zero* (New York: Doubleday, 1992).

community of almost all other nations, those that have suffered significant civilian casualties on their own soil. (In this context the commonly made comparison with Pearl Harbor is interesting: there the casualties were mostly military, and Hawaii was not at the time the "homeland." Pearl Harbor was, like 9/11, an unexpected attack, but it produced a declaration of war between states of the sort that was not possible after 9/11.) On the other hand, the same event is being used to image an outrageous exceptionalism, as if this act has come as a bolt from the blue and not as the latest in a cumulative series of attacks by America on others, and on American citizens, property, and military personnel by others over a number of years—a series that has a complex and discussable (if also debatable) history. The claim of exceptionalism— nothing like this has ever happened—perhaps assists the case for moral equivalence, since the very sign of what is called terror is its radical unpredictability. But surely we have not yet fully suffered with those we saw suffer or, some would say, have made to suffer, and surely this one event cannot stand as absolution for or empirical equivalent to the ravaged places of the world in whose destinies the United States and its allies have been implicated. No more should it be deployed to ease the conscience of those who still think about the rights and wrongs of August 1945. The passage of the term Ground Zero into the common language—for the site will now forever be known by that name—can indeed function reflexively as an indicator of the dialectical and cyclic relation between us and then, the homeland and the faraway place, which is one of the recurrent themes of my narrative. To bring out that relation, however, requires critique, which must work against the simple assumption that victimhood comes from taking the name for granted. Lower Manhattan, in complex and recursive ways, may have a connection to Hiroshima, but the most urgent point to be made is that it is *not* Hiroshima, not *our* Hiroshima, not our price of full admission into the community of global suffering. That recognition was perhaps embodied in the widely publicized fear that the worst might be yet to come.

Returning, then, to the "Portraits of Grief": these are anecdotal obituaries, indeed, but obituaries that must to some degree stand in for the epitaphs that cannot be fashioned in the traditional sense, where the bodily remains and the epitaphic sentiments are in close physical contiguity, as in the inscription on a grave or upon an urn. It is perhaps this contiguity that conventionally licenses the rhetorical conventions of epitaphs toward universalizing reflections; if we know or think we know that the body is there below us, in its particular integrity as a certain body and not another, then we can afford reflections about generalities. Obituaries have usually functioned at a distance from bodies and as more detailed and comprehensive accounts of the lives of the dead, including all the less admirable traits of character for which they are remembered: in some cultures, like that of middle- to upper-class Britain, it can even seem that the primary function of the obituary is the venting of stored-up malice toward the deceased, about whom we can finally spill the beans without fear of reprisal. The epitaph, for the most part, depends on simplicity and philosophical gravity, so much so that its ultimate distillation may well be in complete silence and emptiness. Wordsworth thought so, and on his own gravestone there are simply the dates of birth and death. Some of his most moving poems concern the social dynamics of unnamed graves and memorial landscapes: the fir grove in the poem beginning "When to the attractions of the busy world" and the uninscribed headstones of "The Brothers."[31] Most epitaphs give more than mere dates and names, but they remain committed to simple and general sentiments, only modestly personalized if at all: again, "truth hallowed by love—the joint offspring of the worth of the dead and the affections of the living," as Wordsworth put it.[32] De Quincey, following Wordsworth's lead in his own essay on epitaphs, finds that their language should establish the dead person's "absolute identity with what is highest and lowest, wisest and simplest, proudest and meanest, in all around him."[33] It is this abstraction, this tendency toward the universal, that allows the spectacle of death and burial to open up feelings of kinship and community even with the enemy, the other, as Homer may have intended it to do by his descriptions of the deaths of Priam and Hector (158). Such are the sentiments that Matthew Arnold, in "The Study of Poetry,"

31. I have written on the both of these in David Simpson, *Wordsworth and the Figurings of the Real* (London: Macmillan, 1982), 31–42.

32. Wordsworth, *Prose Works,* 2:58.

33. *De Quincey as Critic,* ed. John E. Jordan (London and Boston: Routledge and Kegan Paul, 1973), 157.

instanced in the three passages of the *Iliad* he deemed indispensable as touchstones for detecting the highest poetic quality: all three dilate the narrative toward understanding mortality as a shared condition, across national borders.

Thus the epitaph, whose location in "modern times" and in the life of crowded towns and cities was already a sign of incipient crisis for Wordsworth in the early nineteenth century,[34] has only become more so in the light of more and more comprehensive techniques for destroying not just lives but the physical bodies that sustained them. In the case of the dead of 9/11, and because there have not been and cannot be many cases in which the established funeral rituals can be gone through, the virtual records of the newspaper columns are playing the roles of both epitaphs and obituaries. Hence perhaps the level of simplification performed by the "Portraits of Grief," so that despite the editorial declaration that these were lives of "unrecountable complexity," what was published was a very simple picture of features common to all. These simplifications were not in the cause of universalizing the experience of death, and they certainly did nothing to inspire gestures of openness to the predicament of the other, the enemy. The component of particularity belonging to the obituary was a nationalized and nationalist one, so that the cumulative effect of reading one after another seemed to come from an editorial interest rather than from any "unrecountable complexity": an interest in the projection of an all-American wholeness of spirit and a national state of health and happiness, and, inevitably, of capitalist neoliberal health and happiness. The universalist potential is supplanted by the national-cultural identity of lives lived in a specific time and place, here in America. Only about two-thirds of the dead of 9/11 are commemorated in the first edition of the *Portraits* (although a second edition in 2003 added four hundred more notices). Most of those who appear there were U.S. citizens living familiar lifestyles (as I have said, those notices about persons with Muslim names and/or from Islamic countries such as Pakistan and Bangladesh tend not to draw attention to matters of religion) ⟨To accept these portraits as self-explanatory, as beyond critique (could one say at "face value"?), is, I think, to endorse a response to these deaths that really does risk

---

34. Wordsworth, *Prose Works*, 2:58.

taking them in vain) It is simply not true that all suffering is for a great cause and leads to ultimate good. These deaths were not for the sake of freedom, even for *our* rather circumscribed version of that concept (of which more later). We have been inundated lately with encomiums to the greatest generation, those who lived through and fought in World War II, and part of the appeal of this memory to us now must surely be that they can indeed be represented as having fought against something for which the word *evil* is more than usually appropriate: Hitler's Nazis, and above all the death camps (whose currency in the national imagination, as Peter Novick shows us, has not always been as high as it is now).[35] There is some likelihood, in this climate of patriotic memorializing, that the dead of September 11 will have their names added to the roster of those who have not died in vain, those who lived freedom and who died for it, not, to be sure, by choice but implicitly, because they loved and enjoyed it as much as they did. They have already been staged as the victims of a war, a war against America, which in turn has authorized a reactive war on what is called terror. Their deaths are paraded to legitimate more deaths elsewhere—the deaths of others as innocent as themselves.

It is in this context that the recourse to the vocabulary of heroism must also be questioned. Rudolph Giuliani's farewell address on leaving the mayor's office in December 2001 is a symptomatic text: "Long after we are all gone, it's the sacrifice of our patriots and their heroism that is going to be what this place is remembered for. This is going to be a place that is remembered 100 and 1000 years from now, like the great battlefields of Europe and the United States."[36] Let us pass over for now, as not requiring comment here, the assimilation of 9/11 to Waterloo and Normandy and Agincourt, and the blithe projection of a thousand-year empire. But let us not pass over the specification of sacrifice, patriotism, heroism. These are all conscious actions and states of mind, things performed or evidenced as the result of decisions made, positions taken, consequences understood. Habermas was sufficiently puzzled by the prevalence of the term in the reporting of 9/11 to wonder whether

35. Peter Novick, *The Holocaust in American Life* (Boston: Houghton Mifflin, 1999).

36. Cited in Nelson and Olin, *Monuments and Memory*, 319.

the word *hero* might have different connotations in American English than it does in German.[37] The hero is the soldier who sacrifices himself to save others, the person who jumps into a flood to save a child. To be sure, some of those involved with 9/11 *were* heroes: the claim may be applicable to many police officers and firemen, and we can surely imagine other forever unrecorded acts of heroism inside the burning and collapsing buildings, akin to those of the passengers who rushed the cockpit of the hijacked plane heading for Washington. Some of these have made it into the record, like Frank De Martini and Pablo Ortiz, Pete Negron, Carlos DaCosta, and others who worked in the building and spent their last moments helping others in obvious disregard of their own safety.[38] But even in the case of the police and fire departments, where devotion to duty in the face of obvious personal danger is surely heroic, the claim to total *choice of self* that Giuliani's rhetoric implies masks the increasingly well-known facts about equipment malfunctions, critical breaks in the chain of command, and sheer incompetence on the part of the authorities and bureaucracies running the response operation, to the point where one wonders whether the word *hero* now means one who need not have died at all rather than (or as well as) one who chose to die for a higher cause than self-preservation.[39]

It is certainly doubtful to the point of implausibility to suggest that anything as rarified as patriotism was in the minds of those dying during the events of 9/11. The multinational (seventy or so nationalities) and multiethnic workforce that was inside the towers on that terrible morning would have subscribed either to a whole range of patriotisms or to none at all. Those who died surely did not think of themselves as dying for their countries, and certainly not

37. Giovanna Borradori, ed., *Philosophy in a Time of Terror: Dialogues with Jürgen Habermas and Jacques Derrida* (Chicago: University of Chicago Press, 2003), 43.

38. See Jim Dwyer and Kevin Flynn, *102 Minutes: The Untold Story of the Fight to Survive Inside the Twin Towers* (New York: Henry Holt/Times Books, 2005), 87–88, 164.

39. Ibid., 248–52, for a quick summary of the cover-up effected by Mayor Giuliani's narrative of heroism. Their book produces a very long list of ways in which disregard for the safety and thus eventually the lives of all of those in the buildings, civilians and emergency workers, was built into the history of the towers and of the emergency services.

for the greater good of the world trade system, whose symbolic identity made them targets in the first place. A few must have died instantly; others had the time to imagine the deaths that they were facing, presumably with a whole range of emotions from sheer terror to some measure of philosophical calm. Most of the recorded last messages that have been publicized were expressions of love. Some jumped, though they have been largely written out of the visual and official memories of the event. Many, perhaps most, must have suffered unimaginable pain from fire and from oxygen deprivation, often in darkness. If this was a sacrifice, it was not one made at the behest of the victims themselves. So we call them at once victims and heroes, those who made a sacrifice and who were the objects of a sacrifice invented by others in the aftermath of their deaths. No one, it seems, will say that these deaths were for nothing, or that the dead have become patriots and heroes by default or by the interpellation of others. Outside the east perimeter of the World Trade Center site during its reconstruction there has been a large board listing the names of the "heroes of September 11, 2001."

The desperate urge to assure us all that these deaths were not in vain, that they were exalted and dignified sacrifices in a great cause, does service to no one—to neither the dead nor the living. It is an inhibition on inquiry, an effort to foreclose attention to the historical circumstances in which they occurred. It masks the disruptiveness and the challenge of 9/11 as calling for ongoing analysis and not for the decisive vocabulary that masks a premature laying to rest. It is conventional to dignify the dead, to disguise any sense that death may be without meaning or purpose. But the conditions that are being thus displaced are different in different times and places, and the matter of identification—not just the names of the dead but the naming of their significance—is one of serious empirical and philosophical concern when their fate is written up in the interests of local and national politics with global repercussions.

This concern can be focused by way of the much-discussed work of Giorgio Agamben, who has argued that it is the capacity to control and dispose of "bare life," human bodies in their minimal condition of sheer or mere physicality, that legitimates and accompanies the power of the state. Agamben's "bare life" is that which cannot be sacrificed but only killed: nothing about it has the required dignity for participation in an act of sacred or legal significance.[40] Bare life stands outside the parameters of citizenship: it is without identity, the exception to all the rules. It is a category that is produced; it does not naturally exist or come to mind of itself but is projected as such within a political-historical formation that requires a group of persons who are without rights or significance, who can be killed with impunity, whose deaths cannot be called a crime. According to Agamben we are now at a moment when the power of the state to declare states of exception and to dispose of life with impunity (as bare life) has increased and is increasing. The totalitarian states of the twentieth century might appear to be things of the past (Hitler and Stalin are no more), but the power structures they devised have been modified as the norms of modern society, so that the concentration camps are no longer exceptional spaces but paradigms for everyday life, "the hidden matrix and *nomos* of the political space in which we are still living" (166). Our biological bodies are now so politically saturated that all rhetorics of simple belonging, whether to nation, culture or community, are undermined.

One could choose to refute or refuse Agamben's analysis on various grounds, and it is certainly something less than a complete or complex empirical description of the way our world is.[41] At worst, it might seem to propose the common suffering of all of us under the umbrella of a paradigm so far limited to the most unfortunate of human beings; this would be a gigantic self-deception. Or perhaps that is what it threatens as the besetting condition of a world still to come. Despite such plausible reservations, the theoretical and metaphorical force of Agamben's model nevertheless remains considerable: the attention now being paid to his work is not accidental or merely hyperbolic. For an understanding of the anxieties and tendencies surrounding the assimilation and commemoration of 9/11, its force is palpable. As I have said, much of the language of commemoration has been seeking to prove that the victims were *not* merely the possessors of bare life but citizens, members of a community governed by ideals and cherished habits and privileged by rights, legally and existentially significant. They were thus, in

40. The exemplary account of the syndrome of bare life is in Giorgio Agamben, *Homo Sacer: Sovereign Power and Bare Life,* trans. Daniel Heller-Roazen (Stanford: Stanford University Press, 1998).

41. For a strong dissent, see Dominick LaCapra, *History in Transit: Experience, Identity, Critical Theory* (Ithaca, NY: Cornell University Press, 2004), 144–94.

Agamben's terms, worthy of sacrifice, and their deaths were accordingly a crime. They died for a way of life and not in vain. Al Qaeda's apparent claim to the power of life and death open to the sovereign state—precisely, to dispose of bare lives—has been countered by the argument that these lives mattered and mattered immensely as embodying all that we hold most valuable and worthy of respect. Thus they are heroes, sacrificial victims, icons of patriotic life, above all saturated with meaning. They connect the present to the past and the future, and enumerating and accounting for their deaths is a national commitment. The state of exception is attached to and identified with the other, the other of terrorism, whose exceptional brutality interpellates our own way of life as hitherto normal but only in the past: it thence authorizes our own deployment of further states of exception, visible both in the technicalities of the Patriot Act and the unjustified invasion of Iraq, as well as in the unprecedented financial payments made to the families of 9/11 victims. Yet by establishing the state of exception as now constant, a condition of unrelenting vigilance in anticipation of a threat that will not now go away (where indeed the worst is said to be yet to come), we have articulated exactly what Agamben has argued is symptomatic of the modern state and of our time, which he sees as marked by the "maximum worldwide deployment" of the state of exception and the consequent conversion of the "juridico-political system" into a "killing machine."[42]

The hyperbole with which it has been proposed that the victims of 9/11 were *not* bare lives, were lives of plenitude and national significance (significance for the nation), becomes then not simply the expected tendency to speak only good things of the dead but also the signature of an anxiety, a hint that we ourselves may be more prone to disposing of bare lives than we should be—the bare lives of those in other parts of the world and perhaps in the midst of our own national plenum, perhaps even the lives of some of the 9/11 victims—the firemen who were not given functioning radio equipment, for example.[43] Efforts to insulate completely the preferred

42. Giorgio Agamben, *State of Exception*, trans. Kevin Attell (Chicago: University of Chicago Press, 2005), 86–87.

43. The case that the United States and its Western allies have been indifferent to their role in the production of impoverished lives is made in Ted Honderich, *After the Terror*, rev. ed. (Montreal and Kingston: McGill-Queen's University Press, 2003).

self from the demonized other, for instance, by the binary pairing of cowardice and heroism, fail to convince or to survive close inspection. To see things this way is not to justify or sympathize with terrorism but to urge a question upon those who too readily assume that it is not something they need to think about in themselves and in their own world sector. Meanwhile, the empty signifier that is "terrorism" cannot be given too much of a place and name if it is to survive as the indicator of an unspeakable and unknowable antagonist: there has, for example, been almost no media interest in the final instructions (essentially a last testament) of Mohammed Atta, who in the eyes of those who share his cause certainly does go by the name of *hero*, and whose last written words it is possible to find moving even in the light of what was to come.[44] It is not just Muslims who have killed or claimed to kill in the name of their god. When a member of the British parliament expressed some understanding of the conditions (not apropos of 9/11) that might have driven her to become a suicide bomber herself, she was removed from her party's front bench.[45]

Much has changed since the days of the (reported) Waterloo bone merchants: the consecration of our own dead has now attained an unprecedented intensity, at least when such intensity is politically useful, while sympathy for the dead of others appears as or more remote than ever. Efforts still continue to recover American human remains from the mountains and forests of South East Asia, the bodies and body parts of 1,800 or so of those missing from the Vietnam War. The effort has expanded to other wars, the Korean War and World War II, and since 1992 ten expeditions a year have been sent to the war zones to find what can be found of the approximately 88,000 undiscovered American bodies.[46] We have the technology to identify and fit a name to even the smallest human remnant, but we also have the technology to create more such remnants or to make bodies disappear altogether. We would not dream of describing those who died for "democracy" as the

---

44. It is reproduced in Bruce Lincoln, *Holy Terrors: Thinking about Religion after September 11* (Chicago: University of Chicago Press, 2003), 93–98.

45. See Jacqueline Rose, "Deadly Embrace," *London Review of Books*, November 4, 2004, 21.

46. Ellen Nakamura, "Slow Homecoming for America's Dead," *Guardian Weekly*, May 13–19, 2004, 36.

scum of the earth, as the Duke of Wellington apparently did, but all too many of them are now indistinguishable from the earth and its atmosphere. The near-total physical destruction that deprives us of bodies to bury is perhaps the material analogue of an enforced denial of materiality itself, since so many of the bodies that have survived—those who jumped or fell from the towers, or the bodies returning from Iraq, for example—have been quietly removed from public sight and thus from a reckoning with the dimensions of time and space involved in their endings. No universal consciousness or sympathy is likely to emerge from that repression, although the lifting of repression is not by any means guaranteed to produce that sympathy. The entire matter of suffering with and for others thus remains in suspension, in ways that are explored later in this narrative. We must look also at the function of photography, such an important part of the "Portraits of Grief," as a genre always premised on the death of its subjects, their being imaged in a past moment, "smaller and clearer as the years go by" in Philip Larkin's memorable phrasing. And what can we say of the prospects for the memorial at Ground Zero? For the Freedom Tower?

2

The Tower and the Memorial

Building, Meaning, Telling

In August 1951 Martin Heidegger gave a lecture in which he responded to the postwar German housing crisis. World War II had seen some 3.5 million homes destroyed, leaving about 7 million people homeless in the homeland. Philosopher to the core, he argued that the perceived problem was not the only problem, or even the real problem: "What if man's homelessness consisted in this, that man does not even think of the *real* plight of dwelling as *the* plight?" Mortals, he supposed, "must ever search anew for the nature of dwelling," which "does not lie merely in a lack of houses."[1] This must have seemed like an almost belligerent refusal to face up to the overwhelmingly empirical needs of postwar German society. One suspects that Heidegger's concern about the metaphysics of humanity's being in the world meant little to those with no roof over their heads, though it might have eased the consciences of those more comfortably accommodated—as if the problem, after all, were not really about bricks and mortar.

1. Martin Heidegger, *Poetry, Language, Thought*, trans. Albert Hofstadter (New York: Harper and Row, 1975), 161. A yet more dyspeptic analysis of the housing situation in the free world had been published by Horkheimer and Adorno, who saw the new suburban bungalows as "at one with the flimsy structures of world fairs in their praise of technical progress and their built-in demand to be discarded after a short while like empty food cans" and thus as subservient to "the absolute power of capitalism." See Max Horkheimer and Theodor W. Adorno, *Dialectic of Enlightenment*, trans. John Cumming (New York: Continuum, 1986), 120.

Nor has a half century of statist caretaking done away with the problem of basic shelter for thousands of Europeans. (Those many Americans who have not benefited from similarly extensive government efforts would seem to be even worse off.) Nonetheless, with the subsequent emergence since 1951 of relative prosperity for more of the Euro-American population, the philosopher's message may now seem less radically insensitive and perhaps even darker as it bids us ponder the limits of successful reconstruction and its indifference to the ultimate quality of life and being. If the problem is not just the lack of houses, then a full supply of them will not solve it.

Heidegger called his lecture "Building Dwelling Thinking." I am cribbing and amending it as my subtitle here to address a topic that seems to me to be implicated in our own state of metaphysical and political health: the rebuilding of the World Trade Center site in Lower Manhattan. Heidegger's apparently dogged indifference to the plight of those actually homeless must seem hard if not impossible to justify, but its useful legacy for the current debate may be the opening of a gap between the immediately obvious and the implicit or possible, between the *now* of an intense historical present, with its seemingly irresistible demands and obligatory genuflections toward usefulness and/or symbolic suitability, and an indefinite historical future, a passage of time of the sort that any major building expects to pass through. Such buildings will, barring disasters, stand firm among strange faces and other minds. They will be workplaces and objects of attention and distraction (though probably not dwellings) for generations to come who do not have a living memory of 9/11. Their coming into being will, like the culture of commemoration in general, draw selectively upon the traditions of the past and represent someone's notion of the present. The buildings that go up on the World Trade Center site are especially recollective in that they will be inevitably memorial, founded in death and in remembrance.

Almost as soon as the towers came down, the debate began about what should go up in their place. It has shown no signs of diminishing as we have moved through a hastily attempted reconstruction plan that was quickly rejected, to an international competition won by Daniel Libeskind, to a heavily modified Libeskind project resulting from the inclusion of David Childs and Skidmore, Owings, and

Merrill, along with the acceptance of Santiago Calatrava's plan for the PATH station, and the selection of a winning design in the competition to build the 9/11 memorial. Most recently, as I write, Frank Gehry has joined the roster. What questions should we be asking of the Libeskind project and its satellites, mutants, and/or counteractive principles as the rebuilding gets under way and starts to particularize and focus the manifold vested interests involved in the passage from concepts to built space? Herder long ago wrote that "the better Gothic architecture is most easily explicable from the constitution of the cities, and the spirit of the times. For as men live and think, so they build and inhabit."[2] Building and inhabiting are likely to remain conflicted and perhaps mutually incoherent at the World Trade Center site. What it will reveal to future generations about the spirit of these times and the constitution of our cities is very much up for grabs. The rush to construction in Lower Manhattan has already proved a fraught and contested process, with all sorts of interests and options kicking in. In this frenzy of discussion and compromise in which the first Libeskind design assumes the status of an original or *Gesamtkunstwerk* from which all other possibilities are imaged either as a welcome improvement or as some sort of fall from or failure of artistic integrity, we still risk forgetting what Baudrillard, taking implicit issue with the Heideggerian assumption, has called "the basic question for architecture, which architects never formulate: is it normal to build and construct? In fact it is not, and we should preserve the absolutely problematical character of the undertaking."[3]

Baudrillard's idea of the normal is hard to specify. He thinks that the mark of good architecture is to "efface itself, to disappear as such," and in a remark whose semiotic ingenuity barely conceals its tastelessness pronounces the destroyed towers themselves "the world's most beautiful building" (52). But he is absolutely right to insist that the September 11 attacks "also concern architecture" (41), and he has written brilliantly on the vanished Twin Towers as icons of cyberculture, "blind communicating vessels" presenting only an opaque face to the outside world,

2. Johann Gottfried von Herder, *Reflections on the Philosophy of the History of Mankind*, ed. Frank E. Manuel (Chicago: University of Chicago Press, 1968), 394.

3. Jean Baudrillard, *The Spirit of Terrorism and Requiem for the Twin Towers*, trans. Chris Turner (London and New York: Verso, 2002), 51.

artificially conditioned and turned in upon themselves, seeing only each other or empty space through those apertures that did exist, their outer skins mimicking nothing so much as "the punch-card and the statistical graph." Above all, their significance consisted in their being *doubled*, in replication on a massive scale as the sign of infinite replicability in a culture increasingly functioning by way of automated replication, a world made up of what is "digital and countable, and from which competition has disappeared in favour of networks and monopoly" (42–43). It was the doubling of the towers that created the opportunity for a second attack identical to the first, thus confirming the image of terrorism as itself opening to an indefinite replication, more and more terror in more and more places. This inextinguishable fear of a terrorism committed to replication of violence then becomes the rationale for instituting a homeland security culture projecting a war that can never end and a state of alert that can never be given over.

Baudrillard's reading of the towers is arresting not least in its attribution of a presumably unconscious or disavowed foreknowledge to the World Trade Center architect, who could not have known clearly or fully, during the design and then the construction years (1966–73), just how aptly these buildings would come to serve as icons of an information culture yet to come into fully developed historical being.

Minoru Yamasaki himself, the architect in question, recorded a very different analysis of his own buildings: "The World Trade Center is a living symbol of man's dedication to world peace . . . a representation of man's belief in humanity, his need for individual dignity, his beliefs in the cooperation of men, and through cooperation, his ability to find greatness."[4] This language is different from that of the Freedom Tower. Humanity, dignity, individuality, greatness—all could come straight from Libeskind's press releases. But not world peace, since what he brought looks rather more like a sword in the raised hand of a militant nation-state. Baudrillard, with the wisdom of a tragical hindsight, does not of course endorse Yamasaki's founding idealism, finding instead an explicit antihumanism in the towers and their significations. They refused the

---

4. Quotation from http://www.greatbuildings.com/buildings/World_Trade_Center.html. See also the citations in Noble, *Sixteen Acres*, 25, 36.

spectator's absorptive gaze while repeating themselves in a self-regard that was exclusive and completely mutual, which might explain why so many New Yorkers hated them in the beginning, and is perhaps the strongest argument in support of those who feel that the best possible outcome of the Lower Manhattan Development Corporation plan would have been to rebuild them exactly as they were—not in response to any desire to defy terrorism and the enemy other, or even to signal infinite resolve (more towers to knock down, more to rebuild, and so on and on), but in recognition of their extraordinarily appropriate meaningfulness as symbols of the world of the late twentieth century and the spirit of those times.

They will not be rebuilt, and it seems that what we will get in *their* place will be an *it*, a singular expression of *something* that will be inevitably retro, a site dominated by one tall tower, and as such a throwback to precisely the culture of competition and of originality (the Empire State Building, Chrysler Building, Woolworth Building). What was called for was an homage to the human spirit and the human identity, so it is no accident that the most uninhibited exponent of this politicized sentimental humanism, Daniel Libeskind, should have been declared the winner in the design sweepstakes. The New York skyline threatens to revert to its traditional iconology of technological triumph, upthrust, and future-oriented optimism even before these buildings have a name. But of course there was no time when they were not named. The name Freedom was there even before a building was imagined.

Before I turn to the topic of the Freedom Tower, it is worth reminding ourselves that towers, especially on this scale, are not natural emanations of a universal human instinct. Before the era of the skyscraper, invented in the United States though now replicated worldwide wherever anyone can afford them, towers (as opposed to domes) are probably best known as features of the great cathedrals and churches of medieval Christianity. We can indeed think of these as phallic and masculinist, but if they are so then it is at the service of a consciously sacred symbolism that sees in the body of the church the shape of the cross and of the body of Christ and thereby of all who believe in him. At least since medieval times towers have also been specified as symbols of pride and improper ambition, although the tower of Babel motif in Genesis is more complicated than that.[5] The medieval tower may thus be taken to signify at once the aspiration to connect heaven and earth and the impossibility of so doing. It resides together with bodily imagery of Christ brought very much to earth. Thus the head lies to the east, with the altar behind it under the east window; the arms mark the transept; the west end stands as the feet (hence perhaps the small doubled west towers on some important cathedrals—the feet of the prone body). We enter by the west door, leaving the world behind us and walking into a historical past that is the source of morning light, returning later to follow our destiny toward death in the setting sun, but now in the knowledge that in our end is our beginning. Thus John Donne's beautiful lines from "Hymn to God my God, in my sickness," almost enough in themselves to make one a believer: "As west and east / In all flat maps (and I am one) are one / So death doth touch the resurrection." Or Wordsworth's fantasy in "Stepping Westward" that "stepping westward seemed to be / A kind of heavenly destiny." In the more complex of the great cathedrals, the main tower is often in the middle of the church, where the nave intersects the transept: the heart of the body. The taller, later Gothic towers, often single in the great medieval churches, tend to stand at the west end, the place of entrance and exit, to which worshipers are summoned by bells. They are encoded not only in a horizontal but also in a vertical symbolism, up to the heavens and down to the crypt, the place of burial. All of these things are habit to churchgoers—habit because mostly unnoticed—but they are intended and coherent, tying together birth, death, and resurrection.

The Twin Towers faced everywhere and nowhere: no east or west windows, no bells, no bodies, and certainly no resurrection. They were perfect and thrilling in their representation of a secularity that went to the limit of refusing the worship of the human spirit itself, notwithstanding Yamasaki's avowed intentions: for

5. The tower whose "top may reach unto heaven" (Gen. 11:4) was being built out of the declared need for a landmark or "name" to use in case the people were scattered—which is exactly what happens, according to God, *because* of the tower. So it is the lack of trust in God that may be at issue here, along with a historical allusion to Babylon (Babel) and a Hebrew wordplay on *balal* (confusion). God does not strike down the tower or the city; they are simply abandoned.

how can there be *two* human spirits? They were, in essence, the cathedrals of our time and place, *all* tower and facing in every direction, but above all inward: nothing *in*human was alien to them. Like the Eiffel Tower, according to Roland Barthes, they made up an "infinite cipher," meaning everything and nothing, a "pure signifier" attracting meaning "the way a lightning rod attracts thunderbolts" but also repelling it, draining away all grand speculations.[6] They were ahead of their time, the product of an apparent disjunction between what Yamasaki thought or said he was doing (did he know more than he said?) and what evolving history came to make of them. The blandness of his prescriptions—peace, dignity, cooperation—seems to have made it possible for the towers to shed or exceed their designated meanings and to accumulate other and more complex attributions with the passing of time, in a process that is still ongoing.

Whatever replaces them can hardly avoid sinking into a morass of signification of the most contrived and hortatory kind. The towers did not speak their names as anything other than the abstraction or virtual reality of world trade. What happens when an "architect" (individual or collective) *tells* us what a building means and tries to short-circuit any discussion of "the absolutely problematical character" of the project? Libeskind has told us, lavishly and in spades, what his design was intended to mean, and I am not the first to find those meanings coercive and reductive, and perhaps also shamelessly opportunistic, whether or not they are sincere, and whatever sincerity means.[7] The potential for metaphysical and architectural defeat in the guise of technological victory has from the first been considerable, because this site has been and remains under pressure to embody both commemoration and rehabilitation, each of which inevitably to some degree undermines the other. Beyond mere rehabilitation, moreover, is the more strident call for triumphalism, for an economic and patriotic display of national and local energy that can pass muster as embodying the spirit of America and, inevitably, of capitalist democracy itself. Far

6. Roland Barthes, *The Eiffel Tower and Other Mythologies,* trans. Richard Howard (Berkeley and Los Angeles: University of California Press, 1997), 2–3.

7. Libeskind's own engaging memoir suggests that this is a man who believes in what he says. See Daniel Libeskind, with Sarah Crichton, *Breaking Ground: Adventures in Life and Architecture* (New York: Riverhead/Penguin Books, 2004).

from resisting or questioning these pressures, Libeskind has seemed to welcome and to exploit them. To be sure, much of the New York skyline took on form as triumphalism and celebration, indeed as explicit advertisement: the Chrysler Building and the Empire State Building were not expected to register moral or historical complexity as part of their program. The World Trade Center site is different. It cannot, given the pressures it responds to, expect to subsist either as a mere memorial or as an uncomplicated icon of economic and cultural suprematism. Many who died were indeed foreign nationals, who imaged a kind of global diversity, but they have mostly not been produced as representatives of a united world consciousness or universal human condition so much as made secondary characters in a distinctly American drama:(hence, I have suggested, one function of the "Portraits of Grief" as emblems of the national lifestyle ideal.)They died as employees of global capital in a place *telling* of its dedication to trade and profit, or, if you prefer, to the civilizing functions of commerce; in place of the gray neutrality of world trade, however, we will now have a freedom whose true and proper home is in the United States. A so-called world building will be replaced by an American building. What architectural signifiers can encompass or finesse this condition as anything other than a more than usually rampant cooptation of complexity by ideology? And how can the celebration or projection of economic revival be made to fit with a recognition of either the dignity or the horror of death and the historical implications of the disaster?

The Lower Manhattan Development Corporation did of course defer the specification of the "memorial(s) within the memorial" to a second phase—another competition, which I discuss later in this chapter. But it is pertinent to remind ourselves that Daniel Libeskind, the architect of the Jewish Museum in Berlin and the War Museum in Salford, England, has already and inevitably made his mark as the "entrepreneur of commemoration."[8] Herbert Muschamp has forcefully taken issue with this project's aspiration toward a pre-Enlightenment religiosity and primitive cosmology cobbled together with a sentimental incarnation of the official

8. Martin Filler's phrase, cited by Christopher Hawthorne, "Living with Our Mistake," *Slate*, February 25, 2003. On Libeskind's Berlin museum, see Huyssen, *Present Pasts*, 66–71.

American way of life; Hal Foster has wondered whether we are in for a new meaning for WTC: the World Trauma Center.[9] But the trauma comes with the triumphal—a conjunction Foster aptly identifies with the German Right after 1918. (The new World War II Memorial in Washington, D.C., has invited similar responses, as we shall see.) The triumphalism is first of all rhetorical, a matter of Libeskind's commitment to language. His project does not merely tell; it shouts. Libeskind describes himself as a storyteller: every building "tells a story," great buildings tell "the story of the human soul"; he set out to design a building capable of "speaking from its stones."[10] This recourse to speech, to voice, to the human soul has all the marks of that culture of "presence" that has been the target of critique for so much of what is called theory (one thinks in particular of Derrida), and stands at obvious odds with the more cerebral and theory-driven projects of some of Libeskind's rivals in the competition for the Lower Manhattan project. The dominating glass shard of his original design (since radically modified) not only visually mimics the arm of Lady Liberty just across the water, but it is to be 1,776 feet high: "Life's Victorious Skyline," replicating the year of the Declaration of Independence. (It also unwittingly reflects the common idea among the site workers that a new tower should represent a finger in the sky, a "giant statue of a hand flipping off the terrorists.")[11] The project subsists by an orgy of nomination: the "Park of Heroes," the "Wedge of Light," the "Garden of the World," "Memory's Eternal Foundation." Perhaps some of Libeskind's coercive and inevitably pastiche coinages will not make it past the prospectus stage— some are indeed already on the sidelines—but others will likely endure. Can we imagine even the most zealous tour guide keeping a straight face as he shepherds his charges to a place proclaiming itself "The Heart and the Soul: Memory Foundations . . . Revealing the Heroic Foundations of Democracy for All to See"? One might think that any democracy requiring this sort of browbeating in the name of architecture must

9. Herbert Muschamp, "Balancing Reason and Emotion in Twin Tower Void," *New York Times*, February 6, 2003; Hal Foster, "In New York," *London Review of Books*, March 20, 2003.

10. Libeskind, *Breaking Ground*, 3–4, 83.

11. See Noble, *Sixteen Acres*, 19–20. Perhaps this is why Governor George Pataki imagined that he might "defiantly reclaim our skyline" (205).

be in deep trouble; indeed, Muschamp finds it "contrary for a place dedicated to democracy to start telling people what to think."[12] Libeskind's soporific doublets are all too coincident with the ideological shorthand of the months after 9/11—giving us, for example, the "axis of evil" and the "coalition of the willing"—which seem to have numbed so many into accepting the case for militant aggression against an Iraqi regime repeatedly associated with the World Trade Center attack but never proven to have had anything to do with it. Whether or not Libeskind's or others' buildings end up with these flagrantly ideological mantras perpetuated on their walls and inscribed on their maps—and there is every chance that some of them will—the political work of the project was being performed long before a single foundation had been poured.

It now seems that much of the energy behind the nomination of the Freedom Tower came from Governor George Pataki, whose purple rhetoric can be found scattered all over the accounts of the debates and discussions about how to rebuild the site. By February 2002 he had invoked "hallowed ground," and the name Freedom Tower has been described as his coinage.[13] He must have seen in Daniel Libeskind a fellow spirit. The effort to peddle the name Freedom actually has a long and occasionally risible history, of which we have very visibly not been reminded over the last three years. In the years around 1800 there was much discussion of new names for the republic, and among the leading contenders was Samuel Latham Mitchill's Fredonia, which would have given us Fredes who spoke Fredish or Fredonian. The result of all of these was a lot of good satirical journalism and some seventeen towns called Fredonia.[14] They would soon be marooned amid a sea of Carthages, Romes, and Athenses, which would then themselves give way to other coinages. The Freedom Tower, in contrast, will stick out like a sore thumb (or raised finger), even as its nomination as such draws upon a definite tradition. On April 19, 2000, President Bill Clinton stood up at the dedication of the Oklahoma

12. Herbert Muschamp, "Ground Zero Rethought, with Judgment Deferred," *New York Times*, September 18, 2003, C13.

13. See Noble, *Sixteen Acres*, 116, 205; Libeskind, *Breaking Ground*, 245. The claim to sacred ground did not, however, go uncontested by some residents of the neighborhood: see Noble, *Sixteen Acres*, 235–39.

14. See Joseph Jones, "Hail Fredonia!" *American Speech* 9 (1934): 12–17.

City memorial and described it as "sacred ground" and as a place "scarred by freedom's sacrifice."[15] This too must stand as a flagrant effort to patch over the divisions within American society revealed by the phenomenon of a former soldier whose act of violence took place in conscious and avowed revenge for the massacre at Waco. Long before, the tomb of the unknown soldier in London's Westminster Abbey, erected after the carnage of the First World War, was inscribed with the hideously disjunctive claim that the multitudes it represents died for "the sacred cause of justice and the freedom of the world."[16] For some time, it seems, there have been no limits on the immodesty of nation-states and their interests in their determination to harvest every possible legitimation effect from the deaths of their citizens.

All architecture of course makes or can be subsumed into some or other political statement simply by being built in a particular place and time. Even the purest abstractions can be chased down to a circumscribed site wherein they are seen to be telling us something. In an identitarian age like our own, in which every aesthetic statement is inspected as the projection of someone's special self or view of the world, these attributions are more pervasive than ever. Even a commitment to the liberating functions of pure form and texture in the abstract-minimal mode risks appearing as highly personal and as nostalgia for something that never was.[17] But it would be worth making the effort, associated—tellingly—with the spirit of *international* Modernism, even while admitting that it may never convince, because what we are seeing is so very different and so alarming: the projection of agreed meanings, assuming the sort of consensus that can only come from totalitarian control or—perhaps the same thing—from a society that really does endorse and tolerate a narrowly limited series of significations and values under the sign of pluralism. Anything built on this site would from the start

15. Linenthal, *Unfinished Bombing*, 234.

16. Edkins, *Trauma and the Memory of Politics*, 24.

17. This was the spirit of Herbert Muschamp's energetic interventions into various phases of the design competitions and review processes: see Noble, *Sixteen Acres*, 121–32, 161–64; and Paul Goldberger, *Up from Zero: Politics, Architecture and the Rebuilding of New York* (New York: Random House, 2004), 116–20. Goldberger's is the best account of the earliest design competition, whose results were dismissed by public and professional opinion; see 93–109.

have had only a very limited chance of generating noncoercive messages: the very occasion of its origin would have made its significations heavily predetermined and inevitably overdescribed. Given the unlikelihood of any low-profile approach to the rebuilding of the World Trade Center site (which I prefer not to call Ground Zero), the most useful polemic to be pursued may well be in the cause of abstraction and unspoken signification.

Libeskind's slogans have added, massively, to this predicament, even as the aggressiveness of his specifications of meaning have been somewhat softened by David Childs's sequence of radical revisions of the design for the tower itself. It is hard to know whether Libeskind just happened to catch the overstated mood of the immediate months after 9/11, and was favored accordingly, or whether he was the well-intentioned tool of interests he could not imagine or control, interests now willing to compromise with the needs and priorities of the leaseholder (Larry Silverstein) and the developers and to climb down somewhat from the high-handed rhetoric of the original site plan. Goldberger bluntly sees in the two years following 9/11 "the use of architecture for political ends, not the use of politics for architectural ends,"[18] and there is much evidence for just that. But the debate has not been totally managed, certainly not among the disputing local constituencies that have taken part in it. The result so far has been that the Freedom Tower's mimicry of the Statue of Liberty is now more muted, with Libeskind's raised arm/glass shard displaced by a shorter spire that might pass (if we did not know where it came from) for a radio tower or, as some have suggested, a toothpick. The skeletal component that many found appealing in the THINK team's rival design for the site has been incorporated into the top of the Skidmore, Owings, and Merrill version of the tower. The design is more stately, less like a human figure, and dallies enough with elegance and understatement that it might even one day rise above its name, although the recent addition of a fortified base was not prompted by aesthetic considerations. Depending on whether one counts the spire, it may be the world's tallest building, or it may not; to have introduced this precise kind of ambiguity is itself a move in the right direction. But for now at least it is still 1,776 feet high (including the spire), and it

18. Goldberger, *Up from Zero*, 256.

is still the Freedom Tower. Governor Pataki was quoted thus at the ceremony unveiling the Skidmore, Owings, and Merrill design: "This is not just a building. This is a symbol of New York. This is a symbol of America. This is a symbol of Freedom."[19] And there will be more freedom to come. The cornerstone (New York State granite, of course) was laid on July 4, 2004. One of the tenants of the World Trade Center site was to be the Museum of Freedom, originally sponsored by American Express and initially designed by Libeskind around "ghost" tracks of the original World Trade Center walkways and the paths taken by the various fire engine companies on their way to the rescue. (Again, the admission that anyone might have died for no good cause or died an avoidable death is inadmissible and thereby everywhere admitted.) The advance politics of this museum are such that its director, a longtime friend of President George W. Bush, has felt compelled to assert that this will not become "a palace of pro-American propaganda."[20] But in its very determination to speak of freedom not just in and for the United States but throughout *the world*, which may be getting a whole floor to itself (New York City may get one too), the Museum of Freedom's board articulates the incredible (but all too credible) presumption of locating this site as the place where the whole world's freedom is on show, open to summary, and at stake.

Could it perhaps be said that this reiterated interpellation of freedom into steel and concrete, this forced marriage between an abstract concept (for what *is* freedom?) and an implacably empirical site, produces evidence of its own absurdity and impossibility? Might it make us wonder whether we really possess this thing that we are struggling so hard to represent, whether we are calling up spirits rather than signifying what is unarguably already there? An honorable strand in postmodern theory tells us that telling is exactly appropriate for our time: Robert Venturi and the coauthors of *Learning from Las Vegas* have made a powerful case for the integrity of a speaking architecture, for buildings that name themselves with knowing reflexivity in the service of demystification and democracy, along the

19. David W. Dunlap, "1,776 Foot Design Is Unveiled for World Trade Center Tower," *New York Times*, December 20, 2003, A1.

20. Robin Pogrebin, "Freedom Center Is Still a Somewhat Vague Notion," *New York Times*, June 24, 2004, B1.

lines of EAT HERE and MOTEL. When we are in a hurry this is what we want: the same might be said of EMERGENCY ROOM and AIRPORT.[21] But these functions do not extend to the memorial site in Lower Manhattan, except perhaps as projections of some future failure of its avowed intentions. The Freedom Tower and its Fredonian affiliates are not (or are not intended as) places for people in a hurry and looking for the most efficient signposts, as places for meeting basic needs. No one, I suppose, is going to come expecting to find and consume freedom. The invitation will be a different one, though in reality it is almost unimaginable that the commercial functions of the World Trade Center site can be held at bay completely; it is an invitation (perhaps more a command) to contemplation. These buildings will demand of us that we "concentrate," that we never assimilate them to a habitual life, that we never forget *that* they mean and *what* they mean. They are not for dwelling, but for dwelling upon, though only within very narrow and prescriptive limits.

Concentration, as I have just used it, is a privileged term, most often taken as the sign of a worthwhile activity that we all ought to cultivate in the face of the anomie and superficial gratification of modern life. Memorials are and perhaps should be sites of concentration; I return to this later. Walter Benjamin gave us a different reading of concentration, however, one very much anticipating the spirit of Venturi and one highly pertinent to the present inquiry. In his great essay of 1936, "The Work of Art in the Age of Its Technical Reproducibility," written in an effort to publicize alternatives to the Fascist subsumption of art and ideology, Benjamin called into question the privileging of "contemplative immersion" or "concentration" as the yardstick of aesthetic response.[22] He argued that the rapt attention demanded of the public before objects designated as art is an instrument of class society, a "breeding ground for asocial behavior" (119), as well as a force of negative self-subjectification. At such moments the observer becomes absorbed in the object, taken out of the stream of experience, prone to select out only spe-

21. Robert Venturi, Denise Scott Brown, and Steven Izenour, *Learning from Las Vegas: The Forgotten Symbolism of Architectural Form* (Cambridge: MIT Press, 1977). There is a good discussion of architecture as textuality in Karsten Harries, *The Ethical Function of Architecture* (Cambridge: MIT Press, 1997), 77–96. Harries, under the auspices of Heidegger, is not well disposed to the linguistic turn in architecture.

22. Benjamin, *Selected Writings,* 3:119.

cial items as worthy of attention (fetishism), and committed to a judgmental disconnection between the aesthetic and the ordinary.

By these means, the subject attributes to itself (and simultaneously denies to others) a depth and seriousness, a spiritual identity that can only work to evade the demands of an immediate and material environment. The space opened to depth and seriousness by concentration must, Benjamin thought, also be the space of ideology at its most potent. To interrupt the flow of one's daily life by standing at the shrine of a meaningful aesthetic experience is to open oneself to a reinforcement of the very social divisions that have built up the shrine to the art object in the first place.

Against this all-too-dominant tendency Benjamin argued for a positive estimate of the quality of "distraction" (*Zerstreuung, Ablenkung*), the very distraction critiqued by high Modernist theory in its contempt for mass culture. Not concentrating, being distracted, still stands for many of us as the sign of a superficial response to life. For Modernists and late Modernists it is in the inattentive moments, the moments of distraction, that ideology does its dirty work. For them, concentration is the mechanism of critique: we must be persuaded to cultivate deep attention if we are to get beyond the corrupted world of habits and appearances. Benjamin proposes the opposite: that it is only in the more superficial moments of distraction that we can assimilate art as part of ordinary life, a tool for living and living with, a familiar item that is not set aside for fetishistic contemplation but is simply "there" for us all, all of the time. Architecture is the most important example of the art of distraction. It is a permanent element in human life because "the human need for shelter is permanent" (120). Buildings are for use as well as objects to look at—the habitual and material function always trumps the independence and sufficiency of the gaze. "Casual noticing" displaces "attentive observation" (120) as buildings subsist through time: what first was new and striking becomes simply part of life.[23]

It follows, then, that buildings that tell us what they mean, or scream at us, and are not simply functional in the way that hospitals

23. All the more so in the twentieth century, which has, for Benjamin, "put an end to dwelling [Wohnen] in the old sense" by means of "its porosity and transparency, its tendency toward the well-lit and airy." See Benjamin, *The Arcades Project*, trans. Howard Eiland and Kevin McLaughlin (Cambridge: Harvard University Press, 1999), 221.

and airports are functional (in that what we most care about is finding them when we need them) are seeking not only to resist the passage of time and the accrual of uncontrolled associations but are also
resisting ever being received in a state of distraction, ever becoming
habitually taken for granted in the way that Benjamin finally specifies as being in the proper spirit of the masses and of a democratic
culture. (Adorno for one was famously grumpy about this argument,
though he misunderstood the concept of distraction, imagining it as
something that in a communist society people would no longer
need.)[24] Memorials and monuments, it must be said, seem to require
concentration and specification. Without the names of the dead and
some account of the occasion of their death, these structures cannot
subsist through time *as* memorials. The memorial component of the
Manhattan site will have to resist, as far as possible, being taken for
granted. This being the case, could one not then argue that the function of the other elements of the site—the tower, the plazas, the
functional spaces—ought to be as free as possible of prefigured significations? Many have sensed Libeskind's strident declarations of
meaning, which resist any inclination we might have to a state of
Benjaminian distraction, to be symptoms of a postmodern neocapi-
talist, world-power ethos that can only honestly subsist as an aggre-
gate of slogans so coercive as to seem self-undermining. The rhetoric,
in other words, laughs at itself. But we do not live in an age of irony,
least of all in relation to 9/11 and to the war culture it has been
deployed to sustain. Libeskind himself takes issue with the values of
"a generation steeped in fashionable irony" and takes pride in seem-
ing "hokey." He is proud to be "a populist, a democrat" and to face
down those critics who defend "an antiseptic world where emotions
can be kept at bay." He is quite clear that the towers had nothing to
do with a repressive world-system but were symbols of a "global
democracy and global freedom."[25] The potential of the Freedom
Tower to function as a self-undermining coinage could only work for
a skeptical elite whose members could well come from any and all of

24. Letter of March 18, 1936, in Ernst Bloch, Theodor Adorno, Bertolt Brecht,
Walter Benjamin, and Georg Lukács, *Aesthetics and Politics* (London: Verso, 1977),
123.

25. Libeskind, *Breaking Ground*, 43–44, 159, 121, 274. One is reminded of the
brief heyday among the best sellers of Jedediah Purdy, *For Common Things: Irony,
Trust and Commitment in America Today* (New York: Random House, 1999).

the social classes and ethnic groups (it is by no means restricted to
educated white liberals), but the building is unlikely—since irony is
by definition exclusive—to appeal to the whole of the population or
to those who manufacture its opinions. Such irony indeed rein-
scribes and reproduces an already existing social division and one
further exacerbated by the aggressive effort to assemble symbols of a
national ideology and to represent it in a bunch of buildings. The
effort to speak for a nation, even for a world, would then by its very
overstatement come to seem a desperate attempt to constitute *as* the
nation (or the world) the various interests or groups that did not
cohere as such before the event commemorated. Freedom unravels
itself under analysis, but the more vocal and powerful factions in
play will not confess to or subsidize that message.

There is still the potential for something better than and different from the Freedom Tower to come into existence, because the
rebuilt World Trade Center site will not be just two buildings, a
memorial and a tower, but a host of others, some yet to be deter-
mined and some already under construction or design. So far the
most interesting and significant of these is the PATH station, the
rebuilt railway hub that was integral to the original World Trade
Center function. Santiago Calatrava's design, already under construction as I write, has deservedly received favorable press both
from the professional critics and highbrows and from the popular
media.[26] Extending on birdlike glass and steel wings 150 feet into
the air while being set 60 feet underground, it is a miniaturized
synthesis of both the upward and downward components of the
site as a whole, part grave site and memorial and part commercial
and civic morale-booster. The bird wings mimic what may never
have been workable in the first place: Libeskind's wedge of light,
here given permanent and far less sententious embodiment. And in
designing a roof that can be open to the elements Calatrava has at
once embodied the "emergency" consciousness that will forever
exist here (opening the roof would let out the smoke from a fire)
and repackaged it as a welcome means of access to the many days
of good weather that make being otherwise underground in New
York such a deprivation.

26. See, for example, Goldberger, *Up from Zero*, 236–40. But Noble, *Sixteen Acres*,
256–58, is less celebratory.

On the evidence so far, and with a Gehry building perhaps to come, the PATH station could be the architectural masterpiece of the World Trade Center site. Calatrava likes railway stations and has designed two others in Europe. He envisages this one as a companion to Penn and Grand Central stations, the other great points of access to the city. Is it significant that railways, emphatically in the national and to some degree in the international imaginary, are throwbacks, images of a technology that was revolutionary in the nineteenth century? No one thinks of Amtrak as the symbol of the contemporary world. The era of the train ended at least a good half century ago, with the rise of the automobile and then of air transportation. The great transcontinental rail experience is now had largely by those with time on their hands and a strong sense of nostalgia, or by those unhappy souls who cannot bear to get on a plane. The train is now the image of slow time, of inefficient passages governed by failing equipment, bad weather, and poor scheduling. So there is something breathtakingly retro about the Calatrava station, which can be taken to indicate at the very least a refusal to cast the train into history; perhaps there is also something futuristic, as if it were announcing the rebirth of a necessary technology, which is indeed, when it works, still the best way to get in and out of Manhattan. At a time when various cities across the United States are regretting the loss of the rail systems they once had and are indeed reintroducing them, is the time of rail travel upon us once again? And if so, does this distinctly foreign, old European architect gesture toward a possible erosion of the exceptionalist and isolationist barriers imposed by the homeland between itself and the rest of the world?

The verve and imagination of Calatrava's allusion to the cultural past as a possible future is intriguing. Over a hundred years ago John Ruskin, in *Seven Lamps of Architecture,* abhorred railway stations, which he regarded as beyond any of the beautifications that architects could or should try to afford. Like many of his Victorian contemporaries he was troubled by the development of the railways and the speeding up of life that they seemed to introduce. No one would henceforth have time or take time; everyone would be in a hurry. The station would then always be "the very temple of discomfort," a place tenanted only briefly by those of us prepared to suffer misery in the short term to get somewhere we want to get to.

In this mood we can never be persuaded to admire anything; better not to waste time and money on trying to make railway stations appealing to the eye.[27] Modern travel is still, as it was for Ruskin, organized predominantly for those of us committed to an economy of haste, to always being in a hurry, but the airport is for us what the railway station was to Ruskin. The aesthetics of *Learning from Las Vegas* was already inscribed, though at that time negatively, into Ruskin's sense of modernity in the mid-nineteenth century, as it was before that in Wordsworth's concerns about the consequences of the fast mail coaches and the improved highways. The railway system that was then the image of hyperkinetic modern life has since come to figure more commonly as the archive of a vanished past. But the past has been very much with us. Both the narrator and the subject of W. G. Sebald's 2001 masterpiece *Austerlitz* spend a great deal of their contemplative and social time in railway stations. Opening in the poetically named Salle des Pas Perdus in Antwerp's Centraal Station in 1967, the novel takes us on a virtual tour of Europe's stations: Lucerne, Paris, Prague, and London all figure as the cognates of the distracted and melancholy imaginations of Austerlitz, the lecturer in architecture, and of the narrator, the displaced German just too young to remember the war. Whereas others hurry through, these two characters *dwell* in stations, which are indeed the most suitable homes for those seeking to trace the doomed journeys of Europe's Jews and other displaced persons. Liverpool Street Station, where Austerlitz eventually realizes that he first arrived on a children's transport and where the narrator passes in and out of London, turns out to be founded upon an ancient burial ground, both literally and atmospherically "a kind of entrance to the underworld."[28] In the railway station, one speaks with the dead and takes on the burden of their deaths as one's own. Perhaps Calatrava's PATH station, with its underground life, will turn out to be the most powerful and persuasive of all the buildings now planned and to come at the World Trade Center site. Its very

27. I owe the citation to Harries, *Ethical Function of Architecture*, 31. In a passage that marks out his own book as inevitably "before 9/11," Harries goes on to make a counterargument for the pleasures of airports and stations as gateways to exotic pleasures and new experiences.

28. W. G. Sebald, *Austerlitz*, trans. Anthea Bell (New York: Random House, 2001), 127–28.

function as embedded in rites of passage between places, in time, and between the upper and the lower worlds, gives it a profundity that may turn out to be beyond trivialization. Here, even as we hurry through, we should be at our most thoughtful; here the condensation of cultures past and present may be at its most dense. This cannot and should not be the Freedom Station.

I come, finally, to the memorial. What is the relation of memorial architecture to triumphalist and heroic nomination, to the telling of meaning? What lessons can be learned from, say, Franco's Valley of the Fallen or Lutyens's Thiepval or Lin's Vietnam Veterans Memorial? What options were open to the winners of the World Trade Center memorial competition, and what constraints does the larger scheme of the site itself place upon them? The Irish Hunger Memorial, with its native grasses, soils, and stone, is not faring too well in the harsh New York winters. What pitfalls and possibilities can we imagine facing those chosen to embody the complex instinctual and ideological feelings and demands at work around the prospect of a memorial to the dead of 9/11? The task is a complicated one by virtue of the sheer density of signification that has already taken up space on the site; it is all the more so because the memorial will not only mark an event but also a grave site—body parts of the victims are in and around the spot where they will be commemorated. It has been proposed that ash from the Fresh Kills landfill might be returned to Ground Zero as the most fitting resting place for the physical remains of the dead; even without this ash, the remains of up to a thousand persons—12,000 body parts with their DNA too badly damaged for current tests—will be preserved inside the memorial in vacuum-packed, freeze-dried form, awaiting possible identification by a technology we do not yet have.[29] In the shadow of the Freedom Tower there will thus subsist a prospect of funereal futures that testifies either to the depth of our attachment to being able to mourn *some* physical remains, however small, or to an image of utopian hyperessentialism on the part of those planning their commemoration. We have come full circle since the

29. Michael Kimmelman, "Finding Comfort in the Safety of Names," *New York Times*, August 31, 2003, sec. 2, p. 1. In February 2005 the medical examiner's office announced that it had at least for the present come to the end of its task of identifying body parts.

Waterloo bone merchants: every fragment of a former human being is now the object of careful preservation.

The materials made available by the Lower Manhattan Development Corporation (LMDC) set forth the limits within which the competitors were to frame their designs. First, they were to "recognize each individual who was a victim of the attacks" of September 11, 2001 (in New York, Washington, and in the Pennsylvania plane crash) and of February 26, 1993 (the World Trade Center bombing that killed six people).[30] There must be a place for housing the "unidentified remains" of those who died, a space for contemplation, and an acknowledgment of those who aided in "rescue, recovery and healing." The whole was to be a statement of "enduring and universal symbolism" that is "distinct from other memorial structures" and that will "convey historic authenticity." Covering letters from politicians and LMDC administrators added injunctions that the values of "liberty and democracy ... must be given physical expression" and that the memorial should not only honor the dead but "reaffirm life itself" (and the "universal ideal" of American freedom) and "celebrate the values that endure, drawing inspiration from its setting in the cradle of American democracy."

The memorial competition, in other words, had already sought to prescribe the messages that the winner should project, and they were eerily coincident with the ones governing the selection of the Libeskind design and with Libeskind's own pronouncements about it. There was the same tension between commemoration and celebration, the same bizarre insistence that the disaster and its implications are at once global and specifically national ("American" values are also "universal"), the same demand that remembering the dead be conjoined with the evocation of an upbeat future. If this were not already an impossibly tall order, then there is the insistence on the memorial's originality and on its inclusion of something of the "historical" record, a signifier of the real. Memorials, however, have a habit of looking like each other, not least because they subsist in a visual culture of conventionalized forms that allow for their identification as memorials in the first

30. The mission statement and guidelines were for a while available at www.wtcsitememorial.org.

place. Anything outside those conventions threatens to look like something other than a memorial. The tradition can be modified and even used "against" itself, refreshing the more tired conventions by subtle shifts of the sort that Maya Lin effected in her Vietnam Memorial. There the tradition of naming the dead that had featured on more than a century of commemorative architecture (countless war memorials, most famously Thiepval, built by Lutyens on the site of one of the bloodiest sectors of the Somme battlefield) is not only taken underground (whereas Lutyens and thousands of village stonemasons had gone upward and therefore transcendental even when avoiding orthodox Christian iconography) but arrayed on a semireflective surface that confronts the beholder with his or her own historical presence and thence with the attendant complexities of self-identification (survival and complicity among them). Lin had to respond to a mandate against making any political statement about the Vietnam War, which was (and indeed remains) a very divisive component of the national culture, indeed so divisive as to call into question what the "nation" is and who gets to be included in it and to benefit from it. Although her memorial is now widely recognized as a masterpiece, we should not forget that it was immensely controversial in its beginnings, that it was funded by public contributions (with much money coming from veterans themselves), that there are two other Vietnam memorials competing for space and attention at the same site, and that it continues to evolve through time as a place for reckoning with the memory and afterlife of the Vietnam War, as is evident in the thousands of items left at the wall, and in its centrality to the POW-MIA movement, whose ongoing energy signifies at the very least a radical cynicism about the priorities of those for whose benefit the "nation" is organized.[31]

It may well be that, as W. J. T. Mitchell has suggested, all monuments are implicated in violence, whether in what they represent (a war, a massive loss of life), in what they image iconographically (the gash in the earth of the Vietnam Wall), or in what they stimulate in the afterlife of public conflict and debate.[32] Like Yamasaki's

31. For a fine account of all of this, see Hass, *Carried to the Wall.*

32. W. J. T. Mitchell, *Picture Theory: Essays on Verbal and Visual Representation* (Chicago: University of Chicago Press, 1994), 378–84.

comments on the concept behind the World Trade Center towers, Lin's recorded remarks on the Vietnam Veterans Memorial are non-confrontational and low key; she reported wanting to "create a memorial that everyone would be able to respond to, regardless of whether one thought our country should or should not have participated in the war."[33] She wanted a memorial that would help people "acknowledge the death in order to move on," that would be "apolitical, harmonious with the site, and conciliatory," and that would "create a unity between the nation's past and present" (33–34). The dead and the missing are listed together, so that everyone has a name whether or not a body came home. The Wall (as it has come to be called) has not of course produced peace and reconciliation, not yet. It has also become the site of an ongoing second-order commemoration made up of items laid before it and regularly collected up for storage as themselves consecrated objects.

Everything surrounding the coming into being of Lin's Vietnam Veterans Memorial was, in other words, congenial to ambiguity and uncertainty—about the rights and wrongs of the war itself, about the class distinctions governing who fought and died in it (the names of the dead are listed without military rank), about the treatment of the survivors. Her minimalist architecture proved to be the perfect medium for the debate to continue, and it is still continuing, refueled by the decade of controversy surrounding the afterlives of the veterans of the Gulf War of 1991. The controversies it generated were not just the result of an accident of history, but with hindsight they can be seen to have been anticipated and invited, albeit in the least melodramatic of ways. Charles Griswold has written very finely on the memorial's carefully crafted allusions to and orientation among the other buildings on the Mall, its mimicry of an open book to be read across a transit between the Washington and Lincoln memorials, and the further implications of its geophysical location.[34] While claiming very little through the realm of speech, the Vietnam Veterans Memorial has accomplished and still accomplishes a great deal of critical cultural work, and it is

33. Maya Lin, "Making the Memorial," *New York Review of Books*, November 2, 2000, 33.

34. Charles L. Griswold, "The Vietnam Veteran's Memorial and the Washington Mall: Philosophical Thoughts on Political Iconography," *Critical Inquiry* 12, no. 4 (Summer 1986): 688–719.

to this that the World Trade Center memorial will inevitably be compared.

The New York site (though not the Pentagon site) images itself as a national and even global project, and one based on events in which the enemy is wholly the *other*, the foreign element that is completely outside and beyond America, even as (we are told) its agents are everywhere and likely to strike again without notice. What thus seems likely to be forgotten or unrecalled is the history of violence within America and between Americans that cannot be commemorated wholeheartedly as a "national" memory, because it remains too divisive. At Gettysburg, only the Union soldiers were at first buried in the graveyard. The Confederate dead were interred some miles away in a place of their own. Gettysburg generated the phrase "sacred ground," used there in 1863 by the president of the Evergreen Cemetery Association.[35] It has become once again familiar (even hackneyed), but this time purified of any allusion to any history of domestic conflict. The Indian removals and exterminations, the traumas of slavery, the history of antilabor violence, and the more recent events known as Vietnam, Waco, and Oklahoma City all now similarly stand to be subsumed within a memorial gesture that can, by the experience of victimhood, finally call itself *national*. Just as al Qaeda has given the United States a monolithic international enemy whose exact identity can be specified or ignored opportunistically by the government of the day, so it has also provided an opportunity for Americans to memorialize themselves as united against forces of evil that come from outside rather than from within. No design that offered explicitly to trouble any of these besetting rhetorics would be likely to be approved; any challenge to the hegemonic language of good and evil will have to be covert and implicit.

How then does Reflecting Absence, the winning design by Michael Arad and Peter Walker presented on January 14, 2004, after having already undergone one major revision, stand up to the pressures around and upon it? At first sight, it seems to fail the test of originality precisely to the degree that it is recognizable as a memorial (many felt that all the finalists' designs looked the same). There are trees (expressing the "annual cycle of rebirth"), water, and the footprints of the towers. The very title of the project, "Reflecting

35. Hass, *Carried to the Wall*, 47.

Absence," mimics and pays homage to Lutyens's great memorial at Thiepval, also composed of names where no bodies could be found, also evocative of an emptiness both physical and metaphysical, an "embodiment of nothingness."[36] Thiepval was in Maya Lin's mind too as she designed the Vietnam Memorial, and Lin has been said to have been Arad's most influential supporter on the jury awarding the contract.[37] Arad is a New Yorker who came out ahead of a global search proudly composed of 5,201 entrants from sixty-three different countries. That said, the memorial is provocative enough to have angered many observers who wanted it to be something else— to tell the story of the events of 9/11, to show more of the twisted girders and burned-out fire trucks, to generate some or other notion of "authenticity." On the evidence we have so far, the memorial will be fully in the Lutyens tradition, purposively devoid of sectarian religious icons and of the hortatory language of some of the original instructions handed down by the LMDC. Its central motif is the double void, and most of its vital parts—the names, the interpretive center, the room for unidentified remains—are underground. Its functions of remembrance will then be carried on in spaces remote from the overbearing visual presence of the Freedom Tower and the Museum of Freedom, with which it promises to be in inevitable and entirely appropriate conflict. Going underground has surely been assisted by the somewhat sentimental technologism attached to the slurry wall as protecting the bedrock of democracy—preserving the sight of this was one of the priorities in Libeskind's master plan and in the LMDC's guidelines for the memorial competition. The fortunate outcome of this, however, is a mandate to go down rather than up, producing a (pagan or neutral) journey to the underworld and not a (Christian, all-American) reaching to the heavens above. If Arad and Walker's plans take final form as currently projected, they may just manage to avoid and even to contest the dominant tone of the site master plan. But the power of their project will come from its explicit self-location in the vocabulary of memorial architecture and not from the uniqueness of these deaths in isolation from all others in other places. Exceptionalism is not in the cards.

36. The phrase is Jay Winter's, in *Sites of Memory, Sites of Mourning,* 105.

37. See Noble, *Sixteen Acres,* 230–55; and Goldberger, *Up from Zero,* 204–34, which stresses Libeskind's unhappiness at the selection of Arad's design.

It is too soon to say exactly what will happen as the building takes form (scheduled completion is for 2009), and some of its effect will depend on what else is built around it. The general reinvention of America by way of the World Trade Center site as a nation more sinned against than sinning already seems inevitable. But Pearl Harbor registered in just this way in 1941, whereas the Pearl Harbor memorial, when it eventually came about (only in 1962), was practically devoid of jingoism: it is a masterpiece of meditative intensity that worthily ranks with Maya Lin's work in Washington. It too looks down, not up. Arad and Walker must in some critical sense *refute* the ambient environment created by Libeskind's and/or Childs's buildings. We are not yet in a position to proclaim how the final assemblage of buildings and memorials will look, how they will relate to each other. Plans will evolve, compromises will be made, outcomes perhaps imposed. Above all, the memorial interpretive center and Museum of Freedom together risk falling into the already dominant and remarkably coherent aesthetic tradition that we might call the *terrorist cluster,* the series of memorials already in place and now even more firmly unified by the negatively charismatic circulation of 9/11 as the *summum* of previous events. A reading of James Young's now classic *The Texture of Memory* makes clear that the late twentieth-century efflorescence of Holocaust memorials has produced a subculture of motifs alluding to one another as well as to the events they signify: broken gravestones, railway lines, emaciated figures. In the case of a "career" memorialist such as Avi Shamir, the duplication of elements is even more marked.[38] This tendency of itself leads to the prospect and project of a postmodern "counter-memorial" commemorative vocabulary richly evident in the controversies about the Berlin Holocaust memorial also written about by Young, who was a member of the LMDC panel of judges.[39] The World Trade Center project as a whole seems, however, already to have preempted most of the options for a deconstructive architecture: irony, skepticism, and above all self-implication are unlikely to

38. James E. Young, *The Texture of Memory: Holocaust Memorials and Meaning* (New Haven: Yale University Press, 1993), 301. Huyssen, *Present Pasts,* 94–109, speculates about a positive function for such duplications in the case of, for example, the Buenos Aires memorial to the *desaparecidos.*

39. James E. Young, *At Memory's Edge: After-Images of the Holocaust in Contemporary Art and Architecture* (New Haven: Yale University Press, 2000).

be welcome here, especially in the memorial segment. Arad and Walker will be received as subsisting within the terrorist cluster, whose prototype is the Oklahoma City memorial and whose companionable form is the Pentagon memorial also dedicated to the dead of 9/11. Their prominent alternative gesture toward the memorial tradition of Lutyens and Lin is thus a counterstatement to that, and promises to set up an interesting and perhaps productively dialectical analysis of the forms of commemoration and their implications for a future national imaginary.

The Oklahoma City memorial at the Alfred P. Murrah Federal Building was inaugurated by President Clinton on April 19, 2000, five years to the day after the bomb that took 168 lives. The interest in punctilious time is also imaged in the archways inscribed with the minutes before and after the attack (9:01, 9:03); a similar idea reappears in Libeskind's now controversial and perhaps already passé "wedge of light" motif in New York. The "footprint" of the Murrah Building is preserved, covered with grass. One hundred and sixty-eight empty chairs commemorate the dead, who are also remembered in biographies in the museum. So too are the survivors, whose "stories" are separately recorded. Personal items are preserved in the museum (one per victim), along with all the objects left at the site or sent in the mail by visitors and sympathizers, including many hats and T-shirts (this is a habit instigated or at least made famous by the Vietnam Memorial).[40] This too is "sacred ground," and here too occurred "events that changed the world" and require a "universal symbol." Here too the commitment to celebration is apparent in the attention paid to the heroism and selflessness of the rescue effort and to the nationwide and protoglobal responses of ordinary people.

It will be difficult for the World Trade Center memorial site to avoid both comparison with and allusion to Oklahoma City, and indeed a pattern is already in place that assimilates a whole series of "terrorist" events to one another in some imagined transhistorical continuum. The special exhibit at the Murrah site (which was to travel to the 9/11 sites starting in September 2003) stages "A Shared Experience." And the Terrorism Institute also created on the site

40. Details of the Murrah Building memorial are taken from www. oklahomacitynationalmemorial.org.

publishes a Web site originating at the Dealey Plaza Museum in Dallas and bringing together Ford's Theater, Dealey Plaza, the Lorraine Motel, Pearl Harbor, Oklahoma City, and 9/11. Recall here also the alacrity with which Netanyahu and other right-wing Israelis identified their own cause with that of the victims of 9/11: Mount Herzl in Jerusalem also has a wall inscribed with the names of the victims of terrorism, which just happened to appear, in the *New York Times* of May 7, 2003 (A3), as a photograph "illustrating" the problems with the Middle East peace process. These assimilations index both repression and expression. The effort to conjure up a coherent and sinister national experience of terrorism of course glosses over the enormous differences between these events and their relative scarcity in our still highly "secure" nation-state, though it can readily be used to justify a paranoid view of history. At the same time, putting these events together cannot but serve as a reminder that, with the exception of Pearl Harbor (hardly terrorism, however aggressively some are now redefining it in that way), all of these other horrors were perpetrated by Americans upon themselves (unless, of course, you think that Lee Harvey Oswald was in the pay of the Russians). It is then a short step to recall not only the enormous precedence of the Waco massacre in the mind of Timothy McVeigh, but all the other unrecorded brutalities and accidents that mark our history, including the unforgettable but strangely now displaced history of human carnage (supposedly 600,000 dead) that marked the course of the American Civil War. McVeigh himself had an eye for historical coincidence and allusion. April 19 was the date of the Waco massacre in 1993, which took place (one hopes with an unintended if bitter irony) on Patriots' Day, the day celebrated in New England and elsewhere in memory of America's first militia.

Oklahoma City, then, is at once an aesthetic precursor (and therefore a challenge to the idea of originality) and a political liability for those who seek to use the 9/11 site as an instance of the degree to which America's enemy has finally been proved to be other than itself: al Qaeda has produced the Arab protagonists that so many had at first assumed to be responsible for the Oklahoma City bombing. Oklahoma City too had its fence turned into a shrine, its design competition, its footprint, its iconic journalism (the fireman holding the dying child), and the shattering aftermath of a radically dislocated community.[41] This was an all-American violence, related to a deeply divisive and wholly national recent history. The fact that the World Trade Center was not destroyed by Americans has opened up the floor to the sort of boosterism of which Libeskind has been accused (quite justly, in my view) and which threatens to overpower the memorial project itself (the memorial within the memorial) with another litany of upbeat paeans to liberty and democracy. The memorial outside the Pentagon in Washington, D.C. (where the "light benches" also echo Oklahoma City) cannot ever be that, for all its limitations in the eyes of critics, because it is implacably subservient to a building needing no introduction and already redolent with unignorable ideological and historical associations. Here the decision to base the memorial design on the exact flight path of the hijacked airplane heading into the building has opened up an interesting dialectic affecting what the memorial is telling and meaning. The likely first response is to see it as imaging an attack from outside on the national fortress, now rebuilt so as to seem as if nothing has happened. But can we also now imagine the sublimation and transmigration of souls through those same walls, against the historical narrative, from inside to outside, somehow reversing the sequence of victim and aggressor and the direction of violence, a reversal also at least imaginable because of the carefully age-graded sequencing of the light benches dedicated to the victims? After all, if the traditionally impregnable walls of the Pentagon have been breached once, in such an unexpected way, why not let the fancy roam and imagine other transformations? The play of light and water then comments ironically and powerfully on the dour *givenness* and intractable signification of the building itself. This way of seeing might not be intended or widely received, but it does at least suggest an unresolved response to the definition and imagination of victimhood that the memorial design, however inadvertently, opens up.

Such openness is not, however, the pattern in the recent history of war memorials in Washington, as evident in the Korean War Memorial's heroic, more-than-life-size figures (dedicated in 1995), and in the controversies over what is widely felt to be a hopelessly reactionary design for the World War II Memorial (which has been

41. All powerfully described and analyzed in Linenthal, *Unfinished Bombing*, upon which I am drawing here.

called both Napoleonic and Fascist)—a design moreover built smack in the middle of the historically and politically important public space that is the Mall—all of which suggests that we are on a collective triumphalist trajectory, within which whatever remains of Libeskind's project will be very much at home. The National Coalition to Save our Mall has lost the fight over the World War II Memorial, and it is notable that in its effort to stop the project it was compelled to resort to a language almost as triumphalist as the opposition in casting the Mall as "our monument to democracy" and "the premier democratic public space in the nation, and indeed the world."[42] But these are words, not things, and there is a world of difference in leaving space for future possible uses and closing it off in ways that cannot be changed and that prevent future possibilities.[43] In the World Trade Center site plan, the civic itself has become monumental; with the World War II Memorial, the memorial may have become monumental at the expense of the civic. It stands as the precise antithesis to the AIDS quilt, which took over the Washington Mall for a weekend only, covering almost exactly but only temporarily the space now taken up by the new memorial.[44] It remains to be seen exactly what space is left in Lower Manhattan for memorial, and what kind of memory it will carry. Buildings that tell are always restrictive. When the stories they tell are simplistic, the prospects for serious memorial are to say the least bleak. The now lamented Twin Towers had in fact a rather complex and conflicted iconographic and ideological personality, brilliantly summarized (as we have seen) by Baudrillard as including the punch card, the digital graph, countability, the end of originality and singularity, monopoly (replication, not competition), the black box (impenetrability), and the figure of globalization itself.[45] What is to come in Lower Manhattan does not so far promise such brave complexity and unwitting honesty. If we are going to end up with the Museum at the Edge of Hope or the Museum of Freedom or some similar coinage, along with the now seemingly inevitable

42. *First Annual State of the Mall Report,* October 14, 2002, available at www.savethemall.org.

43. Ellsworth Kelly's fantasy of "a large green mound" at the site of "Ground Zero" makes a not dissimilar statement; see Herbert Muschamp, "One Vision: A Hill of Green at Ground Zero," *New York Times,* September 11, 2003, B1.

44. See Peter S. Hawkins, "Naming Names: The Art of Memory and the NAMES Project AIDS Quilt," *Critical Inquiry* 19, no. 4 (Summer 1993): 752–79.

45. Baudrillard, *Spirit of Terrorism,* 42–46.

Freedom Tower itself, then we must hope and indeed argue strongly for a more complex and less bullying set of significations to contest their effects. In Calatrava's PATH station we may hope for a profound building. Arad and Walker's memorial at least shows signs of not conforming to the political noise generated by the Libeskind plan and its supporters. In these projects, at least, there seem to be some prospects for an architecture that is more than just a matter of the telling. They will not of course solve the problem of dwelling as Heidegger saw it, since the conditions of their existence and their representational energies are different. No one speaks of putting up a Black Forest Farmhouse at Ground Zero—and no one seriously spoke of it for Germany in 1951 either: this dwelling was always something of a virtual monument. If mere dwelling is not the issue here, still there are a number of other powerful cultural traditions that are very much in play, some of which were for Heidegger behind and within the urge to dwell—the burial and remembering of the dead, the passage between the lower and upper worlds, the metaphysics of transit in all its varieties—and are in themselves capable of resisting or radically qualifying the vapid appeal of boosterism and political declaration. Here is Nietzsche on the subject of monumental history, offering remarks that apply also to the history of monuments:

> Monumental history deceives by analogies: with seductive similarities it inspires the courageous to foolhardiness and the inspired to fanaticism; and when we go on to think of this kind of history in the hands and heads of gifted egoists and visionary scoundrels, then we see empires destroyed, princes murdered, wars and revolutions launched and the number of historical "effects in themselves," that is to say, effects without sufficient cause, again augmented. So much as a reminder of the harm that monumental history can do among men of power and achievement, whether they be good men or evil; what, however, is it likely to do when the impotent and indolent take possession of it and employ it![46]

The best hope for the World Trade Center site is that the name of the Freedom Tower will be forgotten or pass unnoticed. It does not seem likely that this will happen. Hence, among other things, this book.

46.Friedrich Nietzsche, *Untimely Meditations,* trans. R. J. Hollingdale (Cambridge: Cambridge University Press, 1987), 71.

3

Framing the Dead

The "Portraits of Grief" series of snapshots and brief obituaries published in the *New York Times* was one of the first efforts at naming and commemorating the dead of 9/11; the more permanently inscribed list of names at Arad and Walker's World Trade Center memorial will be another. As the dead are named, so they are also framed. *Framing* is a term whose double sense aptly captures the work of culture in both its positive and its less admirable operations. On the one hand, to frame is to give a structure and a context to events that may otherwise be without discursive, memorable, or bearable meaning, incorporating them into a more lasting narrative than the mere moment itself affords. The efforts to remember, commemorate, and inter the dead of 9/11—and all the dead thereafter—belong within this positive understanding of framing, which often has been considered elemental to a civilized life (Any attempt at an understanding of 9/11, its place in history, and its projections for a future will constitute some kind of framing, whether it be through acts of remembering, of reliving, or of critique.)

On the other hand, as we know from movies and crime novels, to *frame* means to set up, to place the blame and the punishment on an innocent person. In this sense also the dead of 9/11, and others, are being framed, exploited for purposes over which they and their families have no control. Just as they were made emblematic of the values and progressive opportunities of a capitalist economy wherein no roads lead to anything but happiness and no future is other than completely rosy, so they have been reimagined and reproduced over the past four years as evidence and legitimation for all sorts of political, military, and commercial purposes, most obviously the war in Afghanistan and its almost seamless transition into the invasion and occupation of Iraq. All those oddly imposed terms such as *heroes* and *sacrifice* and *ground zero* have been parlayed into an unjustified and internationally condemned military and political adventurism that not only arguably dishonors the dead in profound ways but also endangers the living across much of the world. The dead, in other words, have been framed to the purpose of justifying more deaths. The numbers are scrupulously recorded as long as they are American—852 confirmed as of June 29, 2004, the day after the official transfer of power to an interim Iraqi government; 1,182 as of November 15, 2004, the declared ending of the battle of Falluja; over 1,500 by the second anniversary of the invasion in March 2005; over 1,700 in July 2005. Of the Iraqi dead there are no clear records, a fact that casual observers would do well to remind themselves is not to be taken as an indication of some lack of Iraqi piety so much as it is an index of the radical destruction of cultural and bureaucratic continuity—culture itself—that has been visited on Iraqi society. No "Portraits of Grief" for Baghdad, whose civilians are at least as innocent as those who died in America on 9/11. Until well into 2004 the projected figure for Iraqi dead was around 15,000 or fewer, a figure the *New York Times* repeated on October 19. Shortly thereafter a peer-reviewed online essay in Britain's prestigious medical journal *The Lancet* estimated a figure of around 100,000 deaths, half of whom were women and children killed in air strikes. The figures will continue to be disputed even as they subsequently increased significantly after the bombardment of Falluja, the violence surrounding the Iraqi elections, and local bombings and insurrections, which are ongoing.

Meanwhile on June 29, the day after the transfer of power, the *New York Times* published a front-page photograph of a memo passed from Condolezza Rice to George Bush on which the president had written, in heavy ink, "Let Freedom reign!" There is that

---

1. See Lila Guterman, "Lost Count," *Chronicle of Higher Education*, February 4, 2005, A10–13, for an account of the disputes.

freedom thing again. A grammarian would tell us that the sentence is ambiguous; it could be read as a performative ("by this act I pronounce that freedom reigns"), an imperative (perhaps telling Ms. Rice that this will be her job), or a hopeful appeal to higher powers ("let it come about that freedom will reign in the future"). Roll on Fredonia! As it rolls on, or stalls, it is the responsibility of critique to frame the dead in ways that do not underwrite the rhetorical triumphalism and militarism of the United States government and, for much of the time, of most of the media. Such critique must be a key part of any creation of a nondestructive political future, any breaking of the dreary cycle of unnecessary or avoidable deaths. The "Portraits of Grief" was the first but not the last exhibit in the framing of the dead of 9/11. The debate inside the United States has shown and continues to show that there is confusion and disagreement about which parts of the culture of commemoration to invoke and which to ignore in the recording of all the deaths that have occurred since 9/11. It remains an open question whether it is possible to take commemorative procedures out of the hands of the government and its media apologists and to fashion alternative ways to remember the dead and to invoke their deaths in the pursuit of nondestructive ends.

THE MOURNING PAPER

On April 30, 2004, it was mourning in America. The standard newspaper of record, the *New York Times,* registered something of both the muddle and the urgency of the debate about commemoration in its national edition of that day. It did so with a depth and clarity that one might attribute either to a brilliant series of editorial decisions or to the happenstance of journalistic montage as it responded to what turned out to be the news of the day. It was, indeed, the mourning edition, the memorial edition. In Washington, the controversial World War II Memorial had just opened to the public for the first time. The controversy, as we have seen, had been over the placing of the memorial itself—smack in the middle of the Mall, historically and aesthetically a symbol of the right of assembly and the power of assembly—as well as over its design. Its circular array of columns topped with wreaths does indeed smack of an archaic triumphalism, notwithstanding the obligatory fountains and reflecting pool. Meanwhile a small town in Tennessee was trying to preserve what little is left of its Civil War battlefield from the clutches of the developers, partly out of homage to the dead and partly in a commitment to an authenticity of memorialization: people want to walk where others actually died. (The phrase now routinely invoked for the World Trade Center site in lower Manhattan, "sacred ground," was, remember, also used at Gettysburg.) Elsewhere in the newspaper, one learned that the developer of the World Trade Center site had been handed a significant financial defeat by his insurers; that a critical stage had been reached in the case being tried in a Brooklyn courtroom concerning the compensation of Holocaust survivors; and that the planned broadcast of Ted Koppel's television show *Nightline* would be blocked by TV stations in several major cities because his plan to read out the names and show pictures of the American dead in Iraq was deemed by Sinclair Broadcast Group to be unpatriotic and subversive. As if this were not enough, Terry Nichols, the convicted Oklahoma City bombing conspirator already serving a life sentence, was on trial again, this time for his life. The unfinished business of one act of terrorism thus spilled over into the aftermath of the next. The names of two more dead soldiers were published—no pictures—for a total of 718 American dead to date, many more than half of them since the president had declared that the war was over. Also reported were the findings of a study discovering that the number of prisons in the United States had almost doubled since 1974, with Texas leading the way "in a league of its own." Because these prisons tend to be built in rural areas, some counties have more than 30 percent of their population behind bars. Again, a Texas county topped the table, with 33 percent of its residents in prison. Extraterritorial Guantánamo did not figure, as it has failed to figure in so many other ways involving basic accountability: this too had been recently in the news.

In some serendipitous postmodern way, all in fragments but yet with an eerie coherence, the daily paper staged an opportunity for America to meditate on its past, on the deaths of soldiers and civilians in three wars and two acts of "terrorism," on justice, on the obligation to remember and the manner of remembering. All of this on the eve of the first anniversary of President Bush declaring "mission accomplished" in Iraq. There was one more anniversary not mentioned in the *Times:* the anniversary of the final evacuation of Saigon in 1975.[2] Intentional or not, the omission seems significant, for the Vietnam War was the one war that no one in the White House, very few in politics, and very few in the mainstream media wished to remember. Vietnam was arguably the formative war for the debates that are still going on about the treatment of the dead, even as the deluge of World War II remembrances worked to eclipse it from the forefront of attention. The silence speaks volumes.

What lay most immediately behind this flurry of reported mourning and memorialization was presumably the extraordinary uproar of a few days before about the publication of photographs of flag-draped coffins leaving Kuwait and arriving at Dover Air Force Base in Maryland. For fourteen years the Pentagon had had in place a policy of refusing press access to the repatriation of dead military personnel. This initiative of the first Gulf War was famously attributed to the desire to avoid another Vietnam syndrome, in which the wide circulation of images of the dead was held partly responsible for the vigor of the antiwar movement. This reason, of course, was (and is) not the one given. Instead, the claim has been that withholding such images is a mark of respect for grieving families and accords with their own expressed desires. A Senate vote of 54–39 subsequently upheld that policy, with only two Republicans crossing party lines to vote against it, even after vigorous protests from many members of the public and many families whose sons and daughters have died in Iraq. Not everyone finds it a healthy or respectful thing to keep hidden the return of the dead. In January 2005 the Louisiana National Guard, ignoring the Pentagon's request, gave permission to a CBS crew to film the arrival of six flag-draped coffins from Iraq.

The otherwise largely successful suppression of public or media attention to the returning bodies is all the more striking in view of the history of exceptionalism whereby the United States, long before others of its allies, had insisted on the return of the physical remains of its war dead. The British dead in World War I were buried on the battlefields: the huge numbers, the all-too-frequent

2. I too needed to be reminded of this: my thanks to Billy Kelly of Stockholm, N.J., for graciously so doing.

absence of any physical remains that could be returned, the reluctance to "reward" some families and not others or to privilege rank and fortune over relative penury, along with the sense that the dead belonged to the soil for which they fought and where they died beside their comrades, all contributed to a government policy against repatriation. The Whitehall Cenotaph and the tomb of the unknown soldier did symbolic service for all the dead. The French government went back and forth, at first forbidding the exhumation of bodies in battlefield graves for reburial in their home towns and villages, and then—only in 1920—relenting and permitting just that. The United States alone was committed to the wholesale physical return of its dead.[3] This policy has remained in place and governs, for example, the continuing effort, some thirty years after the end of the conflict, to locate the remains of American servicemen killed in Vietnam.

But back to April 30, 2004. A First Amendment activist named Russ Kick had petitioned the Defense Department, under the Freedom of Information Act, for release of the photographs of the coffins of those who were killed in Iraq. To his reported surprise, permission was given, and 361 photos hit the Internet at www.memoryhole.org. The press took the cue, and newspapers all over the country circulated the pictures. The *New York Times* was among them, with one on the front page (but discreetly, in a corner, taking second place to the front and center shot of the *Queen Mary 2* arriving in New York harbor) and one inside. But before the Defense Department released its photos, the *Seattle Times* had published a photograph taken by two Maytag employees loading coffins onto planes in Kuwait. The media discussion following from this event was perhaps the reason for the official release, perhaps not. The two employees were fired (not because of any pressure from government, said the Defense Department), and the pros and cons of showing photographs of the dead became a major talking point across the media.

Except that they were not pictures of the dead. The officially released pictures were not of dead bodies. They were of flag-draped transportation caskets decorously arrayed in the cavernous holds of military transport planes, of the planes themselves landing and

3. I am drawing here from Winter, *Sites of Memory, Sites of Mourning,* 22–28.

standing on runways, of tightly knit groups of uniformed men grouped around white hearses or the back ends of airplanes, or carrying caskets from one to the other. They have the too-far-away and asymmetrically composed look of amateur photographs taken in a hurry by people who cannot get close enough. But they are above all decorous and respectful. They suggest that every possible dignity is here being extended to the fallen. There is nothing here to embarrass either the military or the grieving relatives—for who knows who is inside which coffin among coffins that all look alike in photos that carry no date stamp? Perhaps that is the real scandal, the truth that needs to be hidden from view: that these are not individuals but flag-draped boxes, interchangeable components of a process that functions mechanically in supposed defense of a culture that is obsessed with individuality, but whose efforts to represent individuals end up, as they did in the case of the "Portraits of Grief," all looking the same. Dead men and women are here not arrayed in a form wherein their particular attributes matter or can be seen. Death is indeed always the leveler, but here the sameness of flags and boxes is potentially controversial and reveals the automated functioning both of military life and perhaps of the general culture that it serves. The generalizing function of all rituals of commemoration can be a comfort to those remaining, who are thus assured that their own grief has been shared by others. In this case the timing did not quite assist in such consolations. The columnist Maureen Dowd had just caught Paul Wolfowitz in a serious underestimation or recollection of the number of American dead: he was off by about 30 percent.

Later we would learn a good deal about the rituals and basic procedures attending the treatment of the bodies of dead Americans in Iraq from Dan Baum's *New Yorker* article, which followed two of them from battlefield to burial.[4] Baum described the enormous effort undertaken to restore bodies to the point where they could be recognizable, the routinized behavior of the messengers sent to

4. Dan Baum, "Two Soldiers: How the Dead Come Home," *New Yorker,* August 9 and 16, 2004, 76–85. The same author and magazine had already given us "The Price of Valor" (July 12 and 19, 2004, 44–52), detailing the traumas (sometimes leading to suicide) experienced by American soldiers who had killed the enemy "close up" during the campaign. Baum is one of the few published mainstream journalists to take up the topic of death as it occurs to both killers and victims.

the homes of the families, the care taken over requests for the observance of specific religious and cultural rites, and the offer of a general to attend the funeral. One of the dead soldiers Baum followed was Jewish, the other a citizen of the Philippines who had joined the army to speed up his citizenship application in the United States—the award was made posthumously. Along the way we learn that noncitizens make up some 3 percent of the armed forces, beneficiaries of a policy in place since 1952 and fine-tuned by George W. Bush after 9/11 to speed up citizenship procedures for those on active duty (83). Dead Americans, in other words, are not always Americans. (So too the dead of 9/11, whose diverse nationalities have largely been discounted by the claiming of the event as a uniquely American tragedy.) Baum's words are telling, but his article carried no pictures, no images of the dead.

We have had *some* images of the dead: those internationally circulated pictures of a charred body hanging from a bridge and of a largely vaporized body with only a boot left intact. These were the American "security employees" or "civilian contractors"—the word *mercenary* was never used—whose remains were theatrically displayed after they had been killed in an ambush by Iraqi insurgents/militia/resistance fighters/terrorists (each report's choice of terms tells all). And, on April 30, the television networks carried pictures of naked (and airbrushed) Iraqi prisoners abused and/or tortured (we have yet to be clear on this: the word *torture* is coming to be more commonly accepted in regard to these cases but is also often withheld) by American reservists administering a prison, images apparently so unambiguous that the president and supreme commander himself admitted to finding them disgraceful. I return to these later in this chapter. Images of the Vietnam years had been circulating about the same time: some of them apparently to be trusted—the young John Kerry standing with the crew of his gunboat—others notoriously faked—the young John Kerry on a podium with "Hanoi Jane" Fonda at an antiwar rally. A half hour before midnight on April 30, far from prime time, on Ted Koppel's "The Fallen," the names of the American dead in Iraq were read out and their photographs flashed on the screen, two at a time, about three seconds each, for a half hour or so, interrupted by three rounds of commercials and glossed by Koppel himself as intending "to elevate the fallen above the politics and the daily journalism."

He stressed the program's neutrality, neither for or against the war, but insisted on the right to ask questions. But these were not pictures of the dead, or of death. These were pictures of the living, some smiling and informal, some grim faced under oversized military hats or dressed for graduation from high school (a soldier's average age at death always seems to be about nineteen, whether at the Somme, in Saigon, or in Iraq), mostly men, some women—all now dead.

The full-face frames of *Nightline*'s photographs, many provided by the army and the marine corps, echoed the haunting images of the dead of 9/11, which had dominated the national newspapers after the attack on the World Trade Towers. (The program also inaugurated an ongoing television tradition.) Koppel's narration (unlike Dan Rather's later variation) carried no information—no hometowns, no family members, no hobbies, just names and faces. The *New York Times*'s "Portraits of Grief" went on for weeks and weeks, were reprinted in a hardbound volume, and syndicated in newspapers all over the country. Every face carried a story, and as I have argued, the stories were almost all versions of the same story—happy people, fulfilled in their jobs, fountains of love and charity, pillars of their family and community. The assembled miniature biographies told the story of a flourishing civil society indifferent to race, gender, and economic category. Everyone under the roofs of the Twin Towers was happy and getting happier. They had just become engaged, just found the job they wanted, just got their feet on the ground. The televised photographs of the military dead gave no such sense: only the procession of faces seemed the same. But when the death toll reached a thousand the *New York Times* published as many photographs of the dead as it could find and offered an online supplement containing biographical information.[5] This could hardly fail to conjure up the earlier "Portraits of Grief," thus eerily connecting by commemorative conventions two historical events—the World Trade Center tragedy and the war in Iraq—whose empirical *dis*connection the newspaper itself had been previously compelled to acknowledge in a famous apology. But no nationally syndicated outpouring of grief has so far emerged from the increasing roster of military dead, even though it could and has

5. "The Roster of the Dead," *New York Times*, September 9, 2004, A22–24.

been argued that the deaths on both sides of the Iraqi campaign are no more necessary and no less arbitrary than those of 9/11. This campaign has been successfully marketed as a war, so that the spectacle of violence has apparently been returned to the sphere to which it is supposed to belong, that of combat between nation-states. Evidence that the Iraqi army mostly did not fight was conveniently ignored except as it was conducive to a premature sense that the mission was accomplished.

Around the time of the invasion of Iraq there was also an increased circulation of images and reminiscences of the dead of 9/11. The entire photographic archive had been reprinted (in miniature and without the biographies) in the *Times* on the first anniversary of 9/11. Then, on March 9, 2003, almost on the eve of war in Iraq, fifteen more "Portraits of Grief" were published commemorating those whose families had at first not chosen to participate but had since changed their minds. More full-face photos appeared on March 21, this time of First Marine Division combat troops poised to go into battle, six men and six women, still alive. By March 30 and June 2, the faces were those of the newly dead— along with a photo of a British coffin being unloaded at RAF Brize Norton. The *Times*'s running headnote "A Nation at War" echoed the precursor "A Nation under Attack" that had run in the days after 9/11. In between was the eerie iconographic emptiness of Afghanistan, now largely forgotten.

It is not news that the war for and within culture has often been conducted largely by way of images. Al Jazeera's broadcasts from Iraq have been threatened and often preempted by the U.S. armed forces. Meanwhile in the homeland, again as reported on April 30, 2004, George Bush and Dick Cheney went together to face the 9/11 inquiry commission in a meeting that was not aired to the public but that, according to George Bush, allowed the committee to "see our body language, as well, how we work together." Not so the rest of the country—it was, according to one television anchor, as if the event took place in the eighteenth century, before the advent of modern media culture. The captured Saddam Hussein, briefly fixed in the bright lights of international media attention and looking all too human and defenseless, has more or less vanished from sight. Some images, like those of the planes hitting the World Trade Center towers, were shown over and over again. Others, like those of people jumping or falling from great heights onto the streets below, had been quickly removed from circulation. We know that all images are subject to both direct and self-imposed political, cultural, and ideological control. Private Jessica Lynch, who had the independence of mind to resent the propagandist falsifications of her captivity narrative and the courage to say so, thereafter also quietly disappeared from major-media visibility.

The discussion in the spring of 2004 was almost entirely limited to the rights and wrongs of exposing *our* dead to various kinds of public attention. *Nightline* managed to incur right-wing ire and thus gather to itself the mantle of a certain radical heroism simply by showing pictures and reading names of American dead, completely occluding any reference to the many thousands of others who have perished in Iraq. Equally hard to find were any images of the wounded, those who have come back from Iraq with missing body parts and who would have to face a severely diminished life. Only after the notorious *New York Times* apology, of which more later, would we see a front-page image of a young man learning to use an artificial leg. And even here there is an attempt at sweetening the pill and saving face: these legs are "state-of-the-art devices unavailable to the public."[6] The aim, we are told, is the restoration, as nearly as possible, of life as it was before the loss of the limb. It might seem, one supposes, as if the war had never happened and as if the body had never been attacked. This is, once again, far from death. So too was the weeklong television spectacle of the various phases of the Ronald Reagan funeral in June 2004: here at last, quipped one cartoonist, was a funeral that George Bush would allow reporters to photograph. Almost a year after the *Nightline* controversy the *New York Times* published a series of photographs of the American wounded. These too were decorous, showing intact bodies and faces that were wounded but not shattered or even terminally disfigured. Although the accompanying narrative noted the higher than historic rate of amputations, the main thread of the story was upbeat. The wounded "experience a rapid sequence of carefully choreographed medical treatments" and can be back in

6. Michael Janofsky, "Redefining the Front Lines in Reversing War's Toll," *New York Times*, June 21, 2004, A1.

the United States after four days (compared to forty-five during the Vietnam War).[7]

Before the Abu Ghraib prison photos it had been almost impossible to find in the United States the sorts of images of dead or suffering Iraqi civilians that the rest of the world was seeing—equivalents of Nick Ut's famous Vietnam photo of a girl running screaming from a napalm attack, a photograph thought to have done so much to affect the hearts and minds of Americans during a previous war of which we barely speak but are constantly reminded. The parsimonious use of a few images over and over again—above all of the towers under attack, which in 2004 featured in Republican campaign commercials to the distress and outrage of many who saw them—continued to seem to legitimate a connection between Osama and Saddam that even George Bush has, when pressed, had to disclaim. At the same time that the terrifying end of the Twin Towers was attributed to the other that is terrorism, the many references to Hollywood (and thus to a domestic prescience of the spectacle) spoke to a bizarre prepossession of the image within the homeland (although bin Laden would later release a videotape claiming that the idea came from the sight of the Israeli destruction of Beirut). But it too is not an image of death or of the dead or dying. There have been few of these in the United States after September 11 or from Afghanistan or Iraq since. The late W. G. Sebald speculates in *On the Natural History of Destruction* that one of the reasons for the conspiracy of silence among postwar Germans about their responses to and memories of the bombings of their cities was their sense that criminals and victims could not be comfortably differentiated—that they felt they deserved what had happened.[8] Hence the "well-kept secret of the corpses built into the foundations of our state"—German corpses but also those of the enemy, all created, the Germans felt, by themselves.[9] The implacable recalcitrance of Sebald's prose—like Gert Ledig's before him—registers something of the horror of shriveled corpses, boiling and

7. Lynsey Addario and Johnny Dwyer, "The Wounded," *New York Times Magazine*, March 27, 2005, 24–29.

8. His thesis about the literary silence has, however, been contested by Huyssen, *Present Pasts*, 138–57.

9. W. G. Sebald, *On the Natural History of Destruction*, trans. Anthea Bell (New York: Random House, 2003), 13.

congealed blood, a new underworld of bloated rats and flies, and of the manner of death itself. Whatever this might mean to and for imagined German readers—and here of course there continues an unfinished and perhaps unfinishable debate about acknowledgment and revisionism—there is no doubt of its power to communicate the almost unimaginable horror of both the long drawn-out anticipation of death by weapons of mass destruction and the microsecond—or was it longer?—of unthinkable agony that brings it about. Such capacity to respond cannot, however, be tolerated if war is to be waged without serious opposition against an enemy other; war cannot easily survive the capacity to imagine oneself in the body of the other.

Back in November 2003, at least one American soldier did just that—Sergeant Georg Andreas Pogorny faced a possible court martial for cowardice after experiencing panic at the site of an Iraqi cut in half by machine-gun fire. Pogorny was overcome with what he described as "an overwhelming sense of my own mortality."[10] The most troubling implication of this story is that it appears to be untypical, or at least such stories are not typically reported. Few of those in the homeland are given any materials for imagining themselves in the place and body of the other, even the other embodied by their own soldiers, so threatening is the physicality of death and mutilation felt to be. The Brookings Institute, the Associated Press, and others do their best to keep some tally of the Iraqi dead, but their findings are not deemed newsworthy. The images of 9/11, broadcast worldwide in real time, produced an outpouring of sympathy and identification from the most unexpected quarters. Some of this was assuredly routinized homage to the wounded global behemoth or fantasized identification with a life not led by oneself, but some of it was not. Today we live in a world of largely incommensurate images, some seen on one continent and others in the rest of the world. On the day in January 2005 of President George W. Bush's inauguration to a second term, the *Irish Times* published on its front page a photograph of a screaming, blood-spattered small Iraqi girl whose parents had just been shot to death at a checkpoint in Tal Afar. The tendency toward political isolationism is

---

10. Jeffrey Gettleman, "Soldier Accused as Coward Says He Is Guilty Only of Panic Attack," *New York Times*, November 6, 2003, A14.

reinforced and perhaps significantly enabled by an aesthetic isolationism that allows the debate about images of *our* (American,
coalition) dead to seem like the only debate to be had, and that
then resolves the debate in favor of suppression.

Identification with or sympathy for the sufferings of others has
always been hard to generate. It is even harder when we cannot
face our own. The suppression of press coverage of the coffins at
Dover Air Force Base is one symptom of this. How can such a policy
remain in place and relatively unchallenged? Of course the media
are susceptible to the persuasions and vetoes of power, but successful repression over an extended period of time requires more than
this.[11] Is it because very few of us who are physically comfortable
and intact, or even some of us who have witnessed or undergone
physical agony, really want to confront graphic or harrowing evidence of what violent death is really like, what it does to the
human body? The front-page photograph of the grieving Indian
mother and the dead children who perished in the tsunami, published in the *New York Times* on December 28, 2004, was widely critiqued as distasteful and disrespectful, voyeuristic and perhaps
racist. Here the dead are intact, almost as if asleep. Their tiny bodies
are whole, respectfully laid out in rows, and (saving the infants)
covered with blankets. Horkheimer and Adorno were ruthless in
their speculation about how such images function: "Far from con-
cealing suffering under the cloak of improvised fellowship, the culture industry takes pride in looking it in the face like a man,
however great the strain on self-control. The pathos of composure
justifies the world which makes it necessary. . . . Tragedy made into
a carefully calculated and accepted aspect of the world is a blessing.
It is a safeguard against the reproach that truth is not respected."[12]
Appalling as it might seem to say so, the tsunami of December 2004
figured in U.S. media culture as a natural tragedy, an instance of
*un*avoidable death, even though the opposite could have been and
occasionally was argued (noting, for example, the nonexistence of
early warning systems across the Indian Ocean). Its vivid representation in this form was, inevitably, a safeguard against the reproach

---

11. See Mitchell, *Picture Theory*, 399–405, on the relation of the Vietnam legacy
to the media portrayal of the first Gulf War.

12. Horkheimer and Adorno, *Dialectic of Enlightenment*, 151.

that the truth was not being respected in those other "Asian" locations, Afghanistan and Iraq, where bodies, many of them also children, had for some time been vaporized and shattered beyond recognition by high explosives detonated in the service of democracy. The concern for life and death and its decencies briefly supplanted the near compete lack of such concern for the ongoing deaths and woundings elsewhere, those that were and are unambiguously avoidable. The ultimately painful charge made by the photograph of the Indian mother and her dead children was that the human sympathy here elicited could not but function in the cause of the displacement and repression of so many other instances requiring or deserving the same sympathy.

Ethical philosophers, journalists, and others have discussed the complexities of whether and how to represent death, but so far without solving them. Perhaps no solution should even be desired; all deaths are alike, and all are different and subject to different political opportunisms. We cannot know in advance the limits and consequences of any act of representation, although we should always pay attention to the precedents and traditions that explain such patterns and deviations as arise. Elaine Scarry's important book of 1985, *The Body in Pain*, was, for example, eloquent in its critique of the repressions and displacements that the rhetoric of war traditionally effects. Injury and death are war's purpose, but they come to us as thoroughly redescribed in order to prevent the "reality of suffering" from entering our vocabulary. Everything *except* injuring is reported; the violent destruction of human bodies can even be packaged as the unfortunate by-product rather than the very essence and purpose of war.[13] More recently, Chris Hedges' powerful book *War Is a Force That Gives Us Meaning* spends page after page on the horrible details of what happens to the body when it is the target of modern weapons.[14] Hedges turns to the literary classics in a visibly desperate attempt to both communicate and distract from the unimaginable horror of what he has seen in Bosnia, El Salvador, Iraq (in 1991), and other war zones from which he was

13. Elaine Scarry, *The Body in Pain: The Making and Unmaking of the World* (New York and Oxford: Oxford University Press, 1985), 66.

14. Chris Hedges, *War Is a Force That Gives Us Meaning* (New York: Public Affairs/Perseus Books, 2002).

reporting. His method seems understandable given that what did happen and does happen is almost beyond imagining or describing (though he describes it very well). The problem of describing violent death is a complex one; the genre that almost inevitably comes to hand is that of grotesque realism, a language that is by definition paranormal. This is what Sergeant Pogorny felt and understood: the death of the other and its effect on the self were like nothing he had ever seen or imagined.

The *New York Times* made at least one effort to record the real-time qualities of the deaths of those in the towers on September 11, to get beyond the cartoonlike immediacy of the collapsing towers as an image of instant and insentient destruction. In May 2002 a team of reporters produced a lengthy reconstruction, based on records of phone calls and some personal memories, of what went on in the towers between the impact of the first plane and their eventual collapse.[15] The article led with a close-up photograph of people clinging to ledges and window frames outside the buildings, as if on the point of jumping or falling, as numbers of them did. Remarkably, in over four pages of this minute by minute reconstruction (as in the book that came later), there is very little said of absolute terror, of unbearable pain. Perhaps a sense of decorum has prevailed, and this is reasonable. Or perhaps such things were not in the record and could not be registered there. The brave and loving messages sent out by those who must have known that they would or might soon die are a powerful tribute to the courage of ordinary people in the face of appalling prospects. But the suffering itself we have to imagine, if we can: there is little in the reports that seeks to put it into words. The same indirection marks the avoidance of witnessing in the letters written by soldiers at the front, many of which sound the same as they tell of wanting to be united with their loved ones and offer simple assurances of basic well-being ("I'm OK but missing you all"). Is it that no one wants to tell what it is really like to be in the habitual presence of death? Perhaps no one wants to hear? Is this the simplest and most general reason for the recalcitrance of generations of victims and witnesses to talk about what happened to them

15. Jim Dwyer, Eric Lipton, Kevin Flynn, James Glanz, and Ford Fessenden, "Fighting to Live as the Towers Died," *New York Times*, May 26, 2002, 1, 20–23. This was the precursor to Dwyer and Flynn, *102 Minutes*.

or what they saw? If so, is this impulse to be accepted as respectful of the feelings of those traumatized by horrible experiences? Or should it be countered by a critique that is unwilling to accede to the convenience it affords the vested interests that initiate and organize the deaths of others and the destruction of their means of existence, who want nothing so much as an embarrassed silence? If words alone cannot cope with the reality of violent death's assault on the category of realism itself, what about images?

THE ABU GHRAIB PHOTOGRAPHS

The public appearance in April 2004 of photographs of Iraqi prisoners being humiliated and tortured in the Abu Ghraib prison was not in itself a guarantee of sustained worldwide attention: the Bush administration and the Pentagon, which played down the story until it became impossible to ignore any longer, were clearly hoping or betting that it would go away or be received as just one more item in a contested and unreliable image bank within which one could never be sure that what is claimed as having happened really did happen. The pictures were first shown on television and only gradually made their way into the press, with the *New York Times* bringing up the rear guard—evidence perhaps of Chris Hedges' point that the press "usually does not lead."[16] They were more immediately available in other parts of the world, and especially in the Arab world. But sophisticated readers and viewers everywhere are attuned to the knowledge that photos can be faked—in the same way that the image circulated around the same time of John Kerry sharing a podium with Jane Fonda at an anti–Vietnam War rally in the 1970s had been faked. Every time a picture of Osama bin Laden is produced, there is speculation about whether it is real or as recent as it is claimed to be. Pictures of beheadings arouse suspicion—did this really happen? The falling towers themselves, as many have said over and over again, looked like a scene from a disaster movie: this really did happen but looks as if it didn't. Funerals, dead bodies, mutilated corpses—all can be faked. The editor of the London *Daily Mirror* was forced to resign after printing a photograph of a supposed Iraqi prisoner being urinated on by a

16. Hedges, *War Is a Force*, 22.

British soldier. It was a fake. Pictures do indeed tell stories, but potentially too many of them at once—we cannot be sure which to believe. Susan Sontag has given us a good recent history of faked and staged photographs, noting that "only starting with the Vietnam War is it virtually certain that none of the best-known photographs were set-ups."[17] Even here, one of the best known of all those events, Eddie Adams's picture of a South Vietnamese chief of police shooting a Viet Cong suspect through the head, was deliberately performed in front of journalists (59). It was true but it was staged, so that the particular truth it tells is not quite the truth of simple eye-witness reportage. Barbie Zeliser has chronicled a whole history whereby photographs of the Holocaust and other atrocities were mislabeled, distrusted, believed and then distrusted, distrusted and then believed, and at length often received with little or no response at all.[18] After Timisoara, Jean Baudrillard for one thought that we would never again be able to trust filmic evidence for any atrocity anywhere: everything since would have to be understood as subject to "collective demystification."[19] And yet for some reason, and despite all of this inherited uncertainty, the Abu Ghraib photos were not dismissed as fakes. To be sure, there was an effort by some commentators to describe them as fraternity jokes, just blowing off steam, not really showing any damage being done. But by and large, at once and consistently, and without clear knowledge of what might have motivated the soldiers and guards, these photos were accepted as the real thing. Why so?

The Abu Ghraib photos seem to have punctured both the tradition of suspicion and the even more intractable arousal of compassion fatigue, as well as the temptation to simply turn away from such scenes of death or torture. They seemed to be shock photographs that really did shock, as opposed to those staged with the intention to shock and thereby incurring the viewer's resistance or disbelief.[20] After Vietnam the press corps was severely restricted in what it could

17. Susan Sontag, *Regarding the Pain of Others* (New York: Farrar, Straus and Giroux, 2003), 57.

18. Barbie Zelizer, *Remembering to Forget: Holocaust Memory through the Camera's Eye* (Chicago: University of Chicago Press, 1998).

19. Jean Baudrillard, *The Illusion of the End*, trans. Chris Turner (Stanford: Stanford University Press, 1994), 60.

20. See Barthes, *Eiffel Tower*, 71–73.

record and report from the war fronts in the Falklands, in the first Gulf War, and in Afghanistan. Images did come out—the ghastly "Highway of Death" pictures of a retreating Iraqi column destroyed by air attack, and the triptych of the roadside execution and mutilation by Northern Alliance soldiers of a Taliban soldier in Afghanistan. But they were few. The more negatively objectified the subjects of such photos already were, the more acceptable it seems to have been to show them in states of actual or imminent bodily dismemberment. Everyone knew that the executions of Daniel Pearl and Nicholas Berg, and the suspended corpses of American "security contractors," were staged for international distribution as part of a propaganda machine. This does not mean that they were not horribly real, but it seems that the result of being forced or expected to watch the videos or respond to the photos was that many refused to react in a fully sympathetic or spontaneous way to what they were seeing. The video images were not fully contextualized or explained. There were questions about who the executioners were, about the sound–image matches in the footage, about the time of the events. Given that human beings seem to have been here murdered in public, there was surprisingly little meditation and discussion—and subsequent executions seem not to have raised the attention level.

Perhaps the dynamics and dialectics of observation are at issue here. What happens when one watches someone's death as a narrative sequence? One has to decide whether to commit oneself to witness the event to its conclusion, which invokes the question of one's complicity as a spectator, as the person for whom this act is being performed, albeit as repetition of what has already happened. The past cannot be changed, but it is as if it might be, because filmic time exactly repeats historical time. It is not a comfortable feeling; it is understandable that one might wish to avoid it. Sebald, like Barthes before him, thought that all photographs tended toward death in the minds of those looking at them, so that to look once is to keep on looking: "Nothing is left but looking, an obsession in which real time is suspended while, as we sometimes feel in dreams, the dead, the living, and the still unborn come together on the same plane."[21] When real death is coming or has already come,

21. W. G. Sebald, *Campo Santo,* trans. Anthea Bell (New York: Random House, 2005), 157.

making literal the logic of the obsessive gaze, then what is excusable only as long as it is subliminally oriented toward death may become unavoidably disturbing. As Dominick LaCapra has suggested, the position of mere bystander or objective witness is not easily attainable in the case of "limit-events": there is a temptation to identify either with victim or with perpetrator, and neither is a comfortable option.[22] Against the temptation to overidentify with either there may arise a decision not to look at all, to turn away (a similar dynamic may inform responses to pornography). Even in the 1970s, in the immediate wake of the apparently powerful contribution of photography to ending the Vietnam War, Susan Sontag was well aware that photo images, whether by discouraging contemplation or allowing for too many interpretations, had done "at least as much to deaden consciousness as to arouse it."[23] Photographs alone, she decided, are relatively weak "as a means of conveying truth" (112). They need words, words we can trust: "the contribution of photography always follows the naming of the event" (19). Left to themselves they are "inexhaustible invitations to deduction, speculation and fantasy" (23). In her later book she writes of the meanings of photography as "blown by the whims and loyalties of the diverse communities that have use for it."[24]

What then might explain the peculiar resonance and apparent credibility of the Abu Ghraib torture images? First, they are technologically explicable as the products of amateurs with high-tech home cameras that process images on computers. They have no high finish; in their very posings they are unposed, informal. They do not seem staged to shock, or staged to do anything: one of them apparently functioned as the screen saver image on one of the prison computers. They only came to public notice because one soldier (Private Joseph Darby), troubled by what he saw, slid a disk under the door of an investigator. They are both unofficial and out of the sphere of the press corps; they seem of the people and by the

22. See LaCapra, *History and Memory after Auschwitz*, 41–42.

23. Susan Sontag, *On Photography* (New York: Farrar, Straus and Giroux, 1990), 21. See also Mitchell, *Picture Theory*, 281–322. Nudelman, in *John Brown's Body*, argues that the images of the Civil War dead might have been comfortably assimilated into a tradition of staged postmortem photographs in ways that rendered them less shocking than we might suppose.

24. Sontag, *Regarding the Pain of Others*, 39.

people, though who or what they are for is an open question. They are aesthetically and technologically as surprising as they are upsetting in their content. We have not seen things like this before, or not quite. But they also show us what we already knew: that the torture and abuse of prisoners go on and have gone on everywhere—more and more cases are now coming to light in both American and British zones of activity. We have thus been reminded of what goes on in American prisons on a more or less daily basis; of what happened to Abna Louima in New York City, to Rodney King in Los Angeles, and to many other such unfortunates who fell into the hands of persons with weapons and uniforms. The true focus of our curiosity here is therefore not on the suffering Iraqis, who are unknown to us and can barely be distinguished one from another in these poorly defined and airbrushed images, but on ourselves.

And who are we? Some of us are women, and that too seems to be a first in the annals of "war" photography. The genre of these pictures is that of pornography as well as of violence; in other words their confusions and mixed messages accurately record the contiguity and interdependence of these two genres in the national culture at large—the culture of the homeland. Susan Brison finds them almost indistinguishable from hard-core porn videos available (until recently) on the Web and featuring "real soldiers" and "Iraq women."[25] In the same genre are all the other memories that have come up in the homeland wherein violence and sex are conjoined: the lynchings that were recorded on postcards in the American South; and the evidence produced by Amnesty International for sex slavery in Kosovo, operated by the very NATO troops whose shining moment was declared to have been the liberation of a suffering people in the Balkans War. The intimate alliance between war and the collapse of traditional sexual decorum is well known, or should be: Abu Ghraib once again reminds us of what we already knew. The airbrushing of Iraqi male genitals only dramatizes the existence of the very dynamic it is attempting to conceal, in the same way that airbrushing is intended to dress up hard-core

25. Susan J. Brison, "Torture, or 'Good Old American Pornography'?" *Chronicle of Higher Education*, June 4, 2004, B10. The quotation (a bizarre effort at exoneration) is attributed to right-wing populist Rush Limbaugh.

violent porn as soft porn. The prominent role of women in these images has its own fascination: women leading men on leashes, making fun of male sex organs, organizing torture. Some startled conservatives have tried to use these events to argue against the presence of women in the military, and there was a real risk that these two or three young women would be asked to take the fall for what is quite clearly a systematic and pervasive feature of prison culture both at home and abroad.[26] But as more and more evidence of pervasive torture surfaced, it became clear that scapegoating a few bad apples would not placate world opinion. The Abu Ghraib photos could have a very long shelf life.

What of the pictures we have not seen, the ones viewed by the politicians (some 280 in all) and deemed too upsetting and degrading for release? They have been described as recording male rape, sodomy with blunt objects, and other acts more extreme than the ones we have seen already. As I write, at the beginning of July 2005, over a year has gone by and these pictures have been kept entirely under wraps by legal prohibition and by a conspiracy of silence. They have been seen by senior politicians and by the military leadership but not by the public. One could say that the potential damage to the dignities and reputations of the individuals who were the victims of these acts is itself reason enough to keep them out of circulation. But we have seen how well airbrushing works, and the same techniques that were applied to the first photographs could presumably be applied to the faces and other individualizing features of the prisoners. More plausibly, the motives have to do with an aggressive effort at damage control, a hypothesis supported by various articles accusing the Bush administration of obstructing investigations of Abu Ghraib and similar incidents by playing off the army, the Red Cross, and the Senate against each other and withholding crucial evidence from everyone.[27] It is important that someday we see the rest of these images from Iraq, along with

26. A convenient record of the official and some of the unofficial evidence for this is included in Mark Danner, *Torture and Truth: America, Abu Ghraib, and the War on Terror* (New York: NYREV Inc., 2004); and Karen J. Greenberg and Joshua L. Dratel, eds., *The Torture Papers: The Road to Abu Ghraib* (Cambridge: Cambridge University Press, 2005).

27. See, for example, "Abu Ghraib, Stonewalled," *New York Times*, June 30, 2004, A22.

those from Afghanistan, Guantánamo Bay, and other places where similar things have been going on. The effect of those first photos, however, cannot be duplicated: we now know what has been happening, and further evidence would mostly confirm that we know and what we know. We have the words, or some of them, that go with the images.

The Abu Ghraib pictures are unusual in another way. Susan Sontag, in an essay published both in the London *Guardian* and in the *New York Times Magazine,* noted that it has been common for soldiers to take pictures of the atrocities they have committed—Germans did this after killing Jews—whereas "snapshots in which the executioners placed themselves among their victims are exceedingly rare."[28] There are pictures of German soldiers cutting off the beards of old Jewish men, or standing leering over others scrubbing sidewalks or licking them clean. But the major precursor Sontag produces is the lynching postcards (which were the topic of an exhibition in New York not so long ago), in which smiling crowds of white people surround the bodies of dead black Americans. The conjunction, even were we to go no further, is startling and disturbing. We seem not to be so comfortably distinct from those Nazis (or were they ordinary people?), the enormity of whose crimes has for sixty years been deemed the ultimate expression of the human capacity for evil, those whose behavior has seemed to so many to defy explanation, to call for a language of exceptionalism that would put them in a category of their own—the negative sublime of "Auschwitz," which has often functioned (though not without dissent) as the limit case for any normative ethical theory or historical explanation. Abu Ghraib does not replicate Auschwitz, and there are many distinctions one would wish to make between the two. But it remains the case that these images have brought forth a panic of uncertainty about who "we" are and what "we" stand for. This has not been devoid of a certain cultural narcissism, whereby the damage to the national self-image and public reputation matters a good deal more than the damage done to (mostly innocent) Iraqi prisoners. Nonetheless it has meant that the neat distinctions between them and us, between civility and barbarism, cannot be

28. Susan Sontag, "Regarding the Torture of Others," *New York Times Magazine,* May 23, 2004, 27.

mouthed as confidently as they once were. The war against Iraq was fought according to the principles of American exceptionalism: *we* offer freedom and democracy in a place where there has been only tyranny and mass murder. Abu Ghraib was supposed to be Saddam's prison, the icon of his brutality, not ours. But it has turned out differently, and as it has done so we have been reminded of the darker moments in our own national history— such as those lynching postcards—which are after all not simply to be consigned to a barbaric past from which we have emerged.

The point Sontag makes about the Abu Ghraib photos, that they show "us" *among* "them" rather than the other as simply the focus of an objective gaze, whether of pity or cruelty or something in between, signals not only the complicity between master and slave, and the dependence of the master *on* the slave (one of Hegel's lessons that bears constant repetition), but an insecurity of bearing and purpose that is not fully resolved into critical action. Absurd as it may sound, there is a grain of possible truth in the claims that these soldiers were on a lark, that they failed to understand the seriousness or indeed the reality, the real suffering, they were causing or threatening. Private Lynndie England does not look like a classic torturer so much as a young woman having her picture taken at the fairground next to the sheep with two heads. In her courtroom appearance in August 2004 she indeed claimed to remember the events as "just joking around."[29] These photographs cannot be simply assessed as the icons of an intransigent evil: they are too close to home. Surely many of us can imagine ourselves as impressionable young persons, away in a foreign country for the first time in a heady subculture of bravado and emulation, being tempted to similar actions, especially if they were handed to us as instructions or orders from above? The confusion that these pictures have generated has something to do with the way in which most of them destabilize the genres to which they might be taken to belong. The man whose head is covered with women's panties, the pile of naked men, the man on a leash: these are hard to resolve into single or stable meanings. The piles of bodies do not immediately allude to the famous pictures taken at the liberation of Belsen, though they might have been expected to; instead they project

29. Kate Zernike, "Prison Mistreatment," *New York Times*, August 4, 2004, A8.

some weird confusion of genres—cartoons, live theater, even sculpture—that cannot be readily processed. Only when one puts them into a narrative, whereby, for example, the man with a leash around his neck might be being pulled or those in the pile being beaten, does the full sense of brutality begin to emerge. We have to take time to imagine not just the muzzled dogs standing by their handlers in a still-life pose but straining at the leash to attack the genitals of the prisoners standing naked before them. Then there is the hooded man standing in the Christlike posture on top of the box, with the electric wires attached to his body. This photo above all has become a global icon, reproduced and modified in various ways by artists and propagandists.[30] There are also the pictures of the dead—the man wrapped in plastic film—and those who cannot be identified as alive or dead—the men handcuffed on the floor, one with his underwear pulled down. The picture of the dead body wrapped in plastic strip is very different from the one of a young woman pointing to a man's (now airbrushed) penis. The photo of the smiling young woman giving the thumbs up over the same dead body is different again. All of them call for narratives—how else would one know that the man on the box is not only undergoing stress torture but has been told that he will be electrocuted if he loses his posture? But all of them propose possible narratives, ones we have to compose for ourselves, degrees of brutality prospectively ending in death. Subsequent verbal accounts of these and other tortures have begun to provide a means for the imagining of otherwise unimaginable physical pain. The commemoration of the Iraq War in the eyes of the world is going to include the Abu Ghraib photos among its major exhibits.

Since the pictures were first circulated it has been made unambiguously clear by further revelations that the pattern of torture has been general, that it has been tolerated and perhaps even encouraged by some very high indeed in the chain of command, that it has occurred in all the war zones, and that its specific rituals, while remaining depressingly generic in their modes of extreme violence, are also specifically crafted to cause maximum distress and shame

30. See, for example, Sarah Boxer, "Torture Incarnate, and Propped on a Pedestal," *New York Times*, June 13, 2004, WK 14; and W. J. T. Mitchell, "Echoes of a Christian Symbol," *Chicago Tribune*, June 27, 2004.

for devout Muslims: nakedness before others, touching of the genitals, public sex acts. The Abu Ghraib photos have narrowed the gap between them and us as declared by government propaganda—narrowed it to a point where it ought to have become impossible for George Bush to announce, without being shouted down, that America is engaged in "a war to save civilization itself." There is a good deal less talk now than there was about the conditions under which it might be acceptable to torture prisoners, as if it were possible to compute and control some careful calculus of appropriately dispensable suffering and pain.[31] One finger chopped off? Two?

After Abu Ghraib, and as the full extent of the compliant warmongering supported by the major television networks and many of the newspapers during the build up to the invasion of Iraq became more and more apparent, the *New York Times,* as I have already mentioned, felt obliged to publish an apology for its coverage of events. It seemed to many both too little and too late. The apology appeared on an inside page, hardly a headline, and it soft-pedaled the worst of the newspaper's inadequacies even as it accepted blame for others.[32] Nonetheless, it was a step in the right direction, and after its appearance the emphasis of the newspaper's journalism and also the photo content of the front page changed, though only for a while. We were shown not only the young American soldier with the artificial leg already mentioned (June 21, 2004), but also the upsettingly distraught South Korean parents of Kim Sun Il, executed in Iraq (June 23); Iraqi civilians grieving over the bodies of their dead relatives (June 25); and, most iconic of all, an Iraqi mother standing outside Abu Ghraib prison, eyes closed in grief, holding a photo of the son of whom she has had no news since his arrest nine months previously (June 1, 2004). She even has a name, the ultimate admission of humanity for a newspaper that traded so heavily in

---

31. See, for example, Mark Bowden, "The Dark Art of Interrogation," *Atlantic Monthly,* October 2003, 51–56. Bowden both chronicles the existence of torture and endorses it in a weaker form, "coercion," as something that "should be banned but quietly practiced." Torture is a "crime against humanity," but coercion is acceptable and necessary. It would take a book to unravel the moral obscurities and sophistries of Bowden's position. There are some pertinent and prescient arguments in Slavoj Žižek, *Welcome to the Desert of the Real* (London and New York: Verso, 2002), 102–6. I take up this topic again in chapter 4.

32. "The Times and Iraq," *New York Times,* May 26, 2004, A10.

names after 9/11: Huriyah Jassim Gomar. Her son has a name: Adil. (Even Palestinians too started to be named, for a while.) The image is a potent one. We remember the people standing outside Ground Zero in the early aftermath of 9/11, clutching photos of their loved ones and begging for information. Those images in turn reminded Ariel Dorfman of the mothers of the disappeared in Argentina, standing silently with their photographs of sons, daughters, and husbands, a practice thereafter imitated all over the world, and he found in the resemblance a moment of hope:

> It is an extraordinary recognition of our common humanity that the inhabitants of the most prosperous metropolis in the world, when faced with the infernal dilemma of dealing with the instantaneous and violent disappearance of friends and relatives, whose death could be presumed but not ascertained because of the lack of a body, spontaneously recurred to the same methods of memory and defiance that thousands upon thousands of others from the most remote and often impoverished regions of the planet have invented over the last 25 years to cope with a similar mental hell.[33]

There is indeed, as Dorfman registers, the yet deeper pathos of those who have no photographs to hold, those whose dead were never recorded by a camera. But the common ground is still visible and powerful. We seemed to have come at least one full circle as the image of bereaved Americans after 9/11 was doubled in that of a grief-stricken Iraqi mother whose son had been caught up in a war waged by us for reasons that are becoming more and more transparently dishonest and that have next to nothing to do with the attack on the World Trade Center.

This opening of imagination and attention to the suffering and human integrity of the Iraqi (and Arab) other did not, however, prove lasting. Once the notoriety of the news media's apologies for failing to verify the rationale for the invasion of Iraq faded away, the naming and representation of suffering Iraqis also disappeared from the mainstream: the screaming, blood-spattered child who was seen on the front of the *Irish Times* and across Europe on

33. Ariel Dorfman, "The True 'Desaparecidos,'" *Chronicle of Higher Education,* September 5, 2003, B9.

Inauguration Day did not circulate widely in the United States. On and around Memorial Day, May 31, 2004, readers and viewers in the homeland were treated to endless reruns of and references to D-day, and above all to Omaha Beach, where so many young Americans lost their lives in what we are repeatedly told was a just war. Sixty years after the Normandy landings, no one should begrudge the survivors and the remembered dead the homage they deserve. But Omaha Beach and the protracted coverage of the Reagan funeral were staged (consciously or otherwise) to displace the crisis of representation that had characterized commemorative culture in America since 9/11. Ongoing avoidable deaths that have no describable relation to just wars or to national security continue almost without notice. About two weeks before the second anniversary of the U.S. invasion of Iraq, the list of American dead passed the 1,500 mark almost without comment in the media and (at least as reported) with an eerie silence on the political circuit. The death of soldiers in Iraq is now seldom a headline or even a news item: names appear as if by magic in a small box on the inside pages of the *New York Times,* although one television show does preserve a ritual of naming and a moment of silence. Worldwide demonstrations on the anniversary itself—some 45,000 marched in London—also went largely unreported. Looking back at Howell Raines's account of his finest moments at the editorial desk of the *New York Times* as discussed in chapter 1, one wonders what the current mood might be among the newsmakers and professional opinion mongers. Raines was a proud mourner, and organizer of collective mourning, as well as an apologist for the world of world trade and the all-American upward mobility narrative. His paper received Pulitzer prizes for this. If his culture of mourning and commemoration were ever to extend to people like Huriyah Jassim Gomar—and there are thousands, hundreds of thousands like her—might we be contributing to the making of a better world? Contesting the framing of the dead by those who work, knowingly or not, to exploit them is currently a priority for an understanding of the national culture. Local communities and organizations are doing that, and they deserve wider acknowledgment than they are mostly getting. The American Friends Service Committee's "Eyes Wide Open" installation opened in San Francisco on March 25, 2005, with rows of empty boots representing the American dead in

Iraq, a week or so after Arlington National Cemetery's exhibition of paintings created by artists from photographs of the dead. There continue to be some alternative framings in the news media, but they are not consistently offered. In November 2004 Dexter Filkins followed a marine battalion through the battle of Falluja: out of 150 men, 6 died and 30 were wounded. Not only are they named, but we are told something of how they died, and they died horribly.[34] There is no such attention lavished on the Iraqi dead, but this was a start. We may not have seen the coffins of these young men coming home, but we know something of the physical details of their deaths. The same newspaper on the same day reported (sec. 2, p. 1) on the refusal by some television networks to show Spielberg's movie *Saving Private Ryan* as part of the Veterans Day scheduling. The reason given was foul language; the deeper reason was undoubtedly the graphic violence, the brutal details of death and dismemberment, that made the movie so memorable and upsetting when it was first released. If the United States today is indeed the society of spectacle, then mere exposure to more and more images will not of itself guarantee that a viewer will experience any meaningful sympathy with or for others. The photo-documentary task is not an end in itself—but it is a beginning. We will never know whether we are indeed already numb, or need to numb ourselves, when faced with images of death and duress unless we see them. Only then will we know whether we can pass from seeing them to feeling them, and from feeling them to acting on those feelings.

For Roland Barthes all photographs, however innocent and routine—the picnic, the portrait, the still life—bring about "the return of the dead," just as "every photograph is a certificate of presence." What is present is death: the photograph of something painful refuses to allow us to move on and to "transform grief into mourning" because it is always there anew and in the same form whenever we look at it. The image of a moment lost forever that the photograph records prefigures one's own death, signals one's own mortality.[35] This explanation might seem an implausibly profound

34. Dexter Filkins, "In Falluja, Young Marines Saw the Savagery of an Urban War," *New York Times,* November 21, 2004, A1, 14.

35. Roland Barthes, *Camera Lucida: Reflections on Photography,* trans. Richard Howard (New York: Hill and Wang, 1981), 9, 87, 90.

one for a genre that has been so often distrusted and rendered inane by the sheer scale of reproduction. But it captures some of what resists being received as habitual or dismissed altogether. Can we say of even the most often-inspected "atrocity" photo—the boy with his hands in the air in the Warsaw ghetto, the naked Vietnamese girl running from the napalm—that it has ever been put to rest, out of mind, into the storage locker of merely inert memory? If we look again, really look, are we not still prone to a grief or a disturbance that can preempt previously completed mourning processes? The images from Abu Ghraib, from Dover Air Force Base, from *Nightline*, from 9/11 itself, not to speak of the countless but less commonly shown images of Iraqi deaths, now risk being passed over before their potential for disturbance has been exhausted or in some cases even initiated. Attempts by government and an often compliant media to market these images selectively and to repress some of them altogether should be resisted at every point and in every possible way. Their radical turbulence does indeed require words for the beginnings of full response, but those words do not close off the range of responses called forth. Instead they open the channels for a possible feeling and imagining of what it means to be tortured or to die or to feel the deaths of others. Only if that process commences in some general way can the world's most powerful and destructive military culture begin to be restrained by the popular will. We must argue for more pictures, and more words to go with them, to offer the dead and the dying, all of them, alternatives to the frames so far imposed upon and around them.

So indeed I believe, but there is no basis here for a naive instrumentalist optimism. More pictures? This alone would provide no guarantee that large numbers of far-away people would experience a sympathetic perception of and identification with the suffering body of the other as if it were their own. The problem of stimulating and maintaining critical empathy is immense and may even be insuperable. Carolyn Dean's recent, powerful work about empathy—work that does not take sides on the empirical question but rather documents and explores in great depth the various ways in which we project our self-consciousness about *not* feeling empathy, about being numb—suggests that there are no easy methods for the cultivation of purposive compassion and critical action. To locate the Abu Ghraib pictures as pornography, for example, feeds into the tradition Dean describes in the preexisting Holocaust scholarship whereby the matter of response is suspended by a paradigm that inscribes the viewer (us) as at once victim and perpetrator, feeling too much empathy or not enough, and thus unable to pass into further critical-historical exploration. To resort to the pornography designation (or to accede to it) is then a way of not experiencing or, alternatively, naming the emotions and identifications still potentially pending; it becomes a way of labeling in order *not* to think further.[36] Between condemnation and fascination, the pornographic designation leaves little room for ongoing disturbance and deeper inquiry. The phenomenon is assigned to a genre, and the genre invites a fixed response in accord with one's prefigurative attitudes to it.

If Dean is right, then more and more photos of Abu Ghraib or Guantánamo or Bagram would in themselves make no necessary difference. So too the harrowing prospect of more dead and shattered bodies, whether of Iraqi civilians or of Americans in the field or coming home to Dover Air Force Base, might not in itself educate an unwilling public or its media into critical action. But I have suggested that the mixture of genres in the Abu Ghraib photos does hold at least the potential for disturbing our sense of distance and self-control, and for holding off options for hasty judgments of condemnation or identification. The photographs do not show that we are all monsters, nor do they confirm that the tortures can be blamed on a few morally delinquent soldiers; they open a disturbingly ambiguous territory in between, where the question remains a question not yet resolved and not easy to resolve. Certainly the energy applied to preventing the release of any more such pictures suggests that they are a source of powerful anxiety among the war's supporters and the politicians. We await many other photos besides these: photos of dead women and children, vaporized buildings and ruined cities, the dead and the dying of all

36. Carolyn J. Dean, *The Fragility of Empathy after the Holocaust* (Ithaca, NY: Cornell University Press, 2004), 116–42. Dean also acutely reports on the bystander syndrome, on emotionalism and hyperidentification, and on the theory of besetting Nazi homosexuality as related explanations (that is, pseudo-explanations) of the normalization of withheld empathy in latter-day responses to the history of the Holocaust.

nationalities. These and others like them will not solve our problems simply by their being seen. But they might at least give us a
better and more accurate record through which to begin to face up
to our own complicities and our possible potential for demanding
alternative futures.

There is a troubling moment in *Civilization and Its Discontents* when
Freud speculates that in our attempts to feel ourselves in the position of the other we are always indulging in "the most subjective
possible" behavior.[37] The example he gives is different from what
one might expect. It is not that our relative comfort makes us under-
estimate the pain of the galley slave, the "victim of the Holy In-
quisition," or the "Jew awaiting a pogrom." The opposite may be the
case: our own refined sensibility makes us *exaggerate* the pain of the
other, who is habituated to suffering by "methods of narcotization"
and "special mental protective devices" we have never needed.
Freud ends this discussion with the potentially chilling remark that
"it seems to me unprofitable to pursue this aspect of the problem
any further." Might we conclude, upon pursuing it further, that the
suffering of others is to be regretted less on their behalf (they are
unknowable) than on our own, as we imagine what it would be like
for *us* if we were suddenly put into their positions without the
preparations of habit? Would we thus not risk tolerating the suffering of others because it cannot be known for what it is in itself, and
thereby placing it beyond the sort of computation upon which acts
of redress might be based? Are they suffering as much as we would
if we were them? The dark implications of Freud's example are
there to be pondered, but they do not lead to single or simple conclusions. The privilege of a refined sensibility for imagining pain
may be just as useful an argument for redress as anything based on
the claim to exact knowledge of degrees of suffering (which is, after
all, the sort of scientism that torturers call upon). Furthermore, the
image of a body shattered beyond recognition calls up more than
just a curiosity about pain and its degrees. Here we are in the sphere
of life extinguished and a future life made impossible. That life could
be imagined as just like ours, one of relative privilege in which the
habituation to extreme pain or suffering might never be necessary.

37. Sigmund Freud, *Civilization and Its Discontents,* ed. and trans. James Strachey
(New York: W. W. Norton, 1962), 36.

Photographs of the dismembered, the dead, and the dying will not in themselves change the terms of the culture of commemoration, whose nationalized and mediatized attributes have usually proved more powerful than any claims for common human sympathies or responses. But if any inquiry into these consequential matters is to be other than radically foreshortened, there is a need for more images and more words.

4

Theory in the Time of Death

The title of this chapter may at first strike the reader as an apt and timely acknowledgment of conditions in the homeland after 9/11, where everyone has been made very aware of living within the time of death. It should also, if my argument so far has been at all convincing, cause some discomfort or resistance in that it reproduces something of the very melodrama I have been trying to counter and critique. For has there ever been a time that was *not* the time of death for someone, and in a sense beyond the natural cycle of mortality? Those periods during which our own familiar histories seem to have been dominated by the expectation of peace and security, for example, Victorian Britain or America after Vietnam and before 9/11, were always intricately implicated in variously apparent or displaced violences: Queen Victoria's often-cited "little wars," or the United States' involvement in maintaining or destroying governments in Central and South America as well as in other parts of the world. Everywhere and always, by war and famine, fire and flood, contingency and conspiracy, people have died unnecessary deaths and had their lives cut short long before the playing out of a natural span. There are the spectacular and legendary moments in which humans have destroyed each other in masses, embodied generally by synecdoche: the Somme, Auschwitz. Sometimes what appear to be natural disasters, like many of the African and Asian famines, including the most recent and continuing one in the Sudan, also have contributory causes that are significantly human and political. Then there are the deaths that have resulted from direct and indirect violence inside those nation-states that think of themselves as at peace; poverty, often mediated by categories of race and locality, is a form of violence that can lead very quickly to death. Life expectancy is still far from uniform within the most prosperous countries. Unequal access to the resources of physical well-being, education, employment, and the basic dignity they bestow erodes both quality of life and its longevity. Factor in the arguable dependence of our own relative if uneven prosperity upon the damaged lives led by others in other parts of the world and the entanglement becomes even thicker. In many of these situations the state has behaved with impunity in the disposition of life and death, treating both its own citizens and their enemies or others as objects of what Agamben has called bare life. Why should I announce, with such apparently cheap melodrama, that theory *now* is to be imagined in the time of death?

What, moreover, can be usefully held together under the name of theory? According to various media pundits and to many within the academy, theory is something that is first and foremost over with, a piece of history, something that was alive but is now dead and buried.[1] As such, it denotes an array of mostly French doctrines (or names) associated with the sixties and generally taken to have been mounting a challenge to the humanist subject, the West, the rule of capital, the law of the father—in short, to the establishment. Since the collapse of the Soviet empire in 1989, an event widely held to have put an end to the period of worldwide political rivalry instituted by the French Revolution precisely two hundred years before, it has been common to announce the end of theory, or its pastiche survival as mere obscurantism or narcissistic self-deception. Respectable scholarly inquiries, such as the one titled *What's Left of Theory?* respond to some of the same issues. Is theory always a byword for formalism, and as such always politically irrelevant? Is the return to literature and to traditional celebrations of its depths and possibilities to be read as an aban-

---

1. See, for example, Emily Eakin, "The Latest Theory Is That Theory Doesn't Matter," *New York Times*, April 19, 2003, A17. Various obituaries recording the death of Jacques Derrida in October 2004 took up the same drumbeat.

donment of theory, of which little is then "left," or as a sign that there is still nothing to the "left" of theory, so that its challenges have yet to be negotiated?[2] Terry Eagleton, who made one reputation (and sold a lot of books) as a friendly guide to the underworld of theory, has been making a new name for himself by denouncing it. Theory for him now means, more or less, postmodernism (another mammoth term), which he takes to be nothing more than the emanation of an American identity-politics sustaining itself by way of a denial of mortality and death and a mythology of unlimited self-making.[3]

Theory, however, began life as a foreign body and has not lost that affiliation. Eagleton's perception of theory as something now distinctly American is symptomatic of a much-discussed syndrome whereby, over the last forty years or so, one wave after another of theoretical work in the humanities and social sciences has been felt to have been either passively assimilated or wholeheartedly imported into the American academy. Because some of the superstars of theory have been hired by American universities, it is assumed that their ideas have become thoroughly accepted and admired there, to the extent that Eagleton can now assert with some hope of being believed that theory itself is a code word for the worst of America. What began as foreign and dangerous has, the argument goes, now been domesticated and rendered toothless: to pay part of the salary of a Derrida is to deprive his ideas of any challenge, to float them in the marketplace of a commodity culture wherein all ideas are equal and equally impotent. When theory came upon us, in the company of the civil rights and student movements and the popular resistance to the Vietnam War, it was not only un-American but anti-American, and it encountered enormous resistance in the anglophone world. (The analogue in Britain was a challenge to common sense and transparent meaning.) Now, thanks to thirty years of visible albeit limited hospitality, so the argument goes, it has become part of the establishment it once critiqued, and while its gestures of dissent

2. Judith Butler, John Guillory, and Kendall Thomas, eds., *What's Left of Theory? New Work on the Politics of Literary Theory* (New York and London: Routledge, 2000), viii–xii.

3. Terry Eagleton, *After Theory* (London: Allen Lane, 2003).

continue to appear, they carry or are seen to carry no threat. Once upon a time the hostility to theory as foreign, dangerous, and critical of homeland cultural traditions was deeply felt and widely expressed. It did not gratify the common reader, being both lexically obscure and intellectually difficult. It attacked the assumptions of liberal society both at the philosophical level of the humanist subject and in its politics. Above all it threatened the imaginary integrity of a national culture as just that, as only mythologically national, demanding instead a constant recognition of and engagement with a range of alternatives that we now somewhat reductively know under the name of the "other." Now, it is said, this is all over: we have heard the story theory has to tell and have learned to tolerate or ignore it as the loyal opposition that justifies the ideology of free speech. Or worse still (the Eagleton polemic), it has become an enthusiastic part of what it once beheld and is found wanting.

Yet thirty or so years on, and notwithstanding the welcoming reception that some universities have accorded to some foreign theorists, things have not completely changed, and plenty of evidence for an ongoing alarm or state of emergency about theory can still be found. There are still regular calls for a return to plain speaking and common sense, to a native tradition, to a healthy respect for facts over theories.[4] For Eagleton, death itself is produced as a ready ally in the cause of a common experience, which theory has somehow ignored; for what is more factual, more commonsense, more plainly spoken, than death? Eagleton tells us that theory (which, again, he understands as having mutated into his idea of American postmodernism) avoids death, obsessing itself instead with sex, but a sex decoupled from death and thereby inauthentic, decoupled from life and from any viable radical politics: cultural theory has rid itself of cultural practice.[5] Along with this it has given up on any defensible idea of truth or morality, taking refuge in a cult of irony and reflexivity. Eagleton, replicating

4. For a critique of this habit, see the essays in Jonathan Culler and Kevin Lamb, eds., *Just Being Difficult? Academic Writing in the Public Sphere* (Stanford: Stanford University Press, 2003), which respond to the widely reported "bad writing awards" given out by a philosophy journal. Bad writing is in many cases a covert synonym for theory.

5. Eagleton, *After Theory*, 66.

Daniel Libeskind's case against irony (discussed in chap. 2) calls for a renewed attention to the suffering body as the human core of a revived critique (155ff.): "there is no private entrepreneurship when it comes to flesh and blood" (166). But there is, of course, whether in the medical industry, in the unequal access to life-prolonging and life-enhancing surgeries and technologies (among them food and drink), or in the weapons industry and in the con-tracting out of security operations to private militia in occupied Iraq. What Eagleton means is that there *should* not be such entre-preneurship, that when it comes to flesh and blood we *should* be able to universalize our senses and our intelligence in such a way that we establish a commonality with others who are also made of vulnerable flesh and blood. For him, the illusions of postmodern theory concerning the unimpeded circulation of desire and gratifi-cation (capitalist ideology, in short) are what prevent such identifi-cation. Property binds you to the present and so "cocoons you from death" (184). America, he says, cannot face up to biology, though it is obsessed with the renewable body; it is thus a "pro-foundly anti-tragic society" (186), displaying the limit case of dis-tance from human sympathy because it is also the limit case of the unequal distribution of property, which makes such sympathy possible at all.

This brings us once again to the problem of empathy discussed—and held to be acutely problematic—at the end of the last chapter. Not uncommonly, the turn against theory is accompanied by a renewed case for the power of literature as the medium better suited to our human needs, better able to cultivate the desired sym-pathy or compassionate identification with the demise of physical suffering. The case for reading back through theory to a renewed recognition of the vulnerable body was also the topic of Eagleton's book on tragedy, *Sweet Violence*.[6] There the case was made for the importance of tragic literature as a means of rectifying the state of abstraction brought about by what Eagleton also calls theory. His case is very similar to the more thoroughly worked-out position of Martha Nussbaum (herself one of the crusaders against "bad writ-ing") in a series of books, including *Love's Knowledge, Poetic Justice*

6. Terry Eagleton, *Sweet Violence: The Idea of the Tragic* (Oxford: Blackwell, 2002).

and, most recently, *Upheavals of Thought*.[7] Here too the representation of alternative human lives in fictional form (tragedy, film, the novel) is proposed as the key resource in a revitalized humanities education and able, at least potentially, to keep us from falling into the worst failures of imagination, those suppressing the dignity and vulnerability of others. Literature can teach us that suffering is not avoidable, irrelevant, or good for us and that compassion is an available ingredient of an adequate ethical personality.

Many humanities workers have agreed with Eagleton and Nussbaum in their urgently conveyed sense of the importance of literature for educating a proper citizenry; others, myself included, have questioned the sufficiency of literature in this respect. Neither of them takes up the nagging question posed by Rousseau, among others, of whether the teleological and formal satisfactions of even the most tragical work of art, which is always (for example, in tragic drama) the representation of a disaster rather than the thing itself, might not also work to insulate the reader or beholder from engaging with any real-life event in a fully alert and responsive fashion. (The same question was raised about the uncomfortable prefiguring of the collapse of the Twin Towers by the Hollywood disaster spectacle.) Does the experience of literature inevitably or even plausibly lead us to a compassionate response to the sufferings of others? Is literature the best means by which we can educate ourselves into an appropriately full engagement with the deaths of others? Suppose the function of literature dealing with the distress of the vulnerable body is to make us think that we have *already* witnessed and empathized with the experience written about or performed, so that instead of being educated into a sympathetic response we are driven into habituating it as something already seen, already dealt with, in the way that one gives money to the first homeless person and then feels much less pressure to give to the second and the third? Wordsworth tried to explain why the sight of the "ghastly face" and "spectre shape" of a drowned

7. Martha C. Nussbaum, *Love's Knowledge: Essays on Philosophy and Literature* (New York: Oxford University Press, 1990); idem, *Poetic Justice: The Literary Imagination and Public Life* (Boston: Beacon Press, 1995); idem, *Upheavals of Thought: The Intelligence of Emotions* (Cambridge: Cambridge University Press, 2001). The agenda for theory's encounter with the body in this respect was set by Scarry, *The Body in Pain* (1985).

man surfacing on the lake of Esthwaite did *not* startle or surprise
him:

> And yet no vulgar fear,
> Young as I was, a child not nine years old,
> Possessed me, for my inner eye had seen
> Such sights before among the shining streams
> Of fairyland, the forests of romance—
> Thence came a spirit hallowing what I saw
> With decoration and ideal grace,
> A dignity, a smoothness, like the words
> Of Grecian art and purest poesy.[8]

Wordsworth records this event as a positive instance of the power
of early reading, which accustoms us to sights we have not yet seen
and makes them bearable when we do see them. He too recapitu-
lates the ambivalence at the core of the act of *hallowing,* an act that
seems to respond to a sacredness that is already there while also
suggesting that his response is itself what brings the sacredness into
being, interpellates it out of nothing. The self can encounter these
potentially traumatic events without collapsing. It does not even
need to experience a period of working through; it bears up, and
carries on. But what if the case for human responsive integrity
depends on being vulnerable and prone to collapse? What if we
want to found an ethical personality on such vulnerability? We
would then have to take the position opposite that taken by
Eagleton and Nussbaum: like Rousseau, we would find ourselves
recommending against going to the theater, even against reading
itself. Far from introducing us to the suffering of others, literature is
here the very thing that makes it bearable and open to acceptance
without loss of self and potentially without a fully compassionate
response: I know, I've already read about it. The prefigurative imag-
inative experience makes bearable the shock of the real.

I am not proposing that reading literature must always and nec-
essarily close off compassionate or action-oriented response, but

---

8. William Wordsworth, *The Prelude; 1799, 1805, 1850,* ed. Jonathan Wordsworth, M. H. Abrams, and Stephen Gill (New York and London: W. W. Norton,
1979), 176. I cite from book 5, lines 473–81.

merely that it cannot be assumed to produce it, and that a compelling case has been made that it does not.[9] Finding something
bearable need not of itself lead to a deadening of sympathy, provided that some other order of thinking or feeling supervene to
modify any sense of complacency. Similarly there is no guarantee
that an *un*mediated experience (before and without the literary
imagination) will not lead to a traumatic state that is equally inert
and unable to act. These situations are always contextually sensitive both in the psychoanalytic sense and in relation to mediatized
ideological formations outside the self (which are also part of what
is called the psychoanalytic). Reading literature could then be made
part of an education in empathy, or used against it, and perhaps
both at the same time for different individual reading subcultures.
There are no preestablished guarantees. The important lesson to be
learned here is that the polemical antithesis proposed by Eagleton
between an experience of literature (as healthy) and a mere reading of theory (as ideological) cannot survive close inspection.
Theory is no more or less productive in any intrinsic sense of good
or bad effects than is literature; to assume that it is replicates, as a
formal category, a division of discourse that is contingent and historical. In the current situation, the affiliation of theory has been
once again strongly marked as foreign, nonnative, and threatening—a figure of terror. This is no time to enlist in the campaign
against theory; it is theory that offers an important alternative
understanding, outside the neoliberal consensus, of what may be
entailed in moral vigilance and moral action.

THEORY BEYOND THE SPECTACLE

The young Wordsworth standing on the shore of Esthwaite and
seeing the drowned man has by way of his literary experiences
already seen in his mind's eye what he is now seeing in reality; he
has already bestowed a protective aura of "decoration" and "ideal
grace" upon the data of new experience, the "fact" of a man's
death. The same prefigurative rationale governed those infamous

9. For a longer discussion, see David Simpson, *Situatedness; or Why We Keep
Saying Where We're Coming From* (Durham, NC: Duke University Press, 2002),
117–45.

responses to the collapsing towers on September 11 in which people announced that it was just like a movie they had seen. It is hard to be clear about what this means: is it a moral failure or a pardonable need for self-reassurance that responds to disaster as something already seen? How does one distinguish, can one distinguish, between ideological and/or aesthetic co-optation by images and a compulsive need to normalize what is otherwise unbearable and perhaps unintelligible? Does the prefigurative artifact confirm the reality of what is before one's own eyes, or dilute it? Could it do both at once? Karlheinz Stockhausen's expression of a sophisticated version of this opinion got him into a good deal of trouble.[10] Are the drowned man and the falling towers instances of what we call, after Baudrillard, the *simulacrum*, the sign without a signified, the image emptied of any connection to the real? Is their preexistence in the world of romance and fairy tale or of the movies enough to deprive them of the power of identification and purposive shock, the power to move and move to action? Are we trapped by the repetition of the spectacle as a commodified form able to digest whatever associates with it in the realm of new experience, making such experience never new and never shocking?

Baudrillard, one of the exponents of what is called theory, had engaged with these questions before 9/11 and pursued the argument to the point of apparent absurdity in his infamous contention that the 1991 Gulf War did not take place. This aggressively counterintuitive statement was widely reproduced as an instance of the silliness and even the moral turpitude of theory—for how can we say that a war in which at least 100,000 people died in the military phase alone did not take place? But Baudrillard's point is a serious one. The war was conducted by and represented to the victors as if it were a glorified computer game directed by remote control from afar and involving no American casualties worth listing. Apart from the horrible photos of the "highway of death" that appeared during the final phases of the Iraqi retreat from Kuwait, there were hardly any images of combat or its consequences for the violated bodies of

10. For an incisive discussion of the controversy, see Frank Lentricchia and Jody McAuliffe, *Crimes of Art and Terror* (Chicago: University of Chicago Press, 2003), 6–14. A convincing case is here made for understanding the attacks on the towers as performance art made with the "co-operation of American television" (13).

its victims. We had seen it all before in video games. (A similar video culture of Iraq-based "real" combat games was generated during the 2003 war and circulated during the "real" time of the invasion.) The minimal numbers of American dead meant that for those in the homeland who were the targeted readers of Baudrillard's sardonic narrative, the war never had to be removed from a purely virtual existence: everything took on the status of information, just as information technology itself operated the weapons apparently without human instigation. In a pattern that repeats itself across the reported experiences of 9/11 and the invasion of Iraq, the hyperbolic insights of Baudrillard's theory are borne out by the empirical record: one young man spoke for many in his assertion that the 1991 war really did not happen: "We don't know anyone who went, no Americans got killed, we didn't see any Iraqis get killed. . . . It's not a part of the history of our time for a whole generation of people."[11] So too the drowned man of Esthwaite did not fully happen for the young Wordsworth, because it had already happened. So too the towers, whose falling bodies and shattered human remains were subsumed by the visual power of a spectacular event, an event that indeed happened twice but is reduced in memory to a single image, the collapse of *a* mighty tower. The power of replication is that it is always one.

Baudrillard saw in the first Gulf War evidence that the power of images worked to flatten all information to the point where it might be true or not true, real or not real: "just as everything psychical becomes the object of interminable speculation, so everything which is turned into information becomes the object of endless speculation, the site of total uncertainty. We are left with the symptomatic reading on our screens of the effects of the war, or the effects of discourse about the war."[12] Nothing can be fully denied or fully believed, every item of information is just that, an item of information. This commits us to an epistemology of fantasy and paranoia in a world in which anything could or could not be true. Thus one Iraqi bystander interviewed about one of the bombings

---

11. Cited in Susan D. Moeller, *Compassion Fatigue: How the Media Sells Disease, Famine, War and Death* (New York and London: Routledge, 1999), 45.

12. Jean Baudrillard, *The Gulf War Did Not Take Place*, trans. Paul Patton (Bloomington and Indianapolis: Indiana University Press, 1995), 41.

in occupied Iraq on June 14, 2004, claimed to believe that the
Americans had set off the bomb themselves because they did not
want to see Iraq become a stable and self-sufficient country. The
forty-two who died in the bombing of a desert compound during the
previous month were either members of a foreign militia infiltrating
Iraq's borders (the American commanders' version) or the unfortunate members of a wedding party (photo and video evidence provided by the survivors). The saturation of all reporting with the
sense of radical uncertainty makes operable the bait-and-switch
manipulations that have had such massive consequences since 9/11.
It makes possible the substitution of Iraq for al Qaeda, and the production of a Saddam who always did and did not have weapons of
mass destruction, an instability successfully cultivated in the face of
the complete absence of evidence that he did have or was about to
have such weapons. We don't know, and we don't know what we
don't know. He might, or he might not. And because he might not,
therefore he might.[13] And what if . . . and what if . . . ? What if the
whole Iraq affair were nothing more than a red herring, a device for
radically transforming the internal political culture of the homeland
(19)? Operation TIPS, the scheme for a national system of citizen-
manned mutual surveillance described by Žižek (55–57) would have
us all watching our neighbors for suspicious signs of terrorist behavior. What if the effect of the invasion of Iraq were the creation of a
fundamentalist regime (home base for terrorism) that did not exist
(Saddam's state was relatively secular) but whose preexistence (as
the home base for terrorism) was assumed and invoked as precisely
the occasion for the invasion in the first place? What if something
similar were to happen in the homeland? In a world in which the
world's major power invades Iraq in order to punish a Saudi multi-
millionaire operating out of Afghanistan (or somewhere else, or
already dead), everything seems plausible. The Arab terrorist at first
widely presumed to have been at work in Oklahoma City has after
9/11 at last been refigured and located, but only in the one place
where he almost certainly was not: Iraq.

13. I am alluding to the famous string of hypotheticals, almost worthy of a
Wittgenstein, uttered by Donald Rumsfeld and taken up as an object of both right-
ful ridicule and telling analysis by Slavoj Žižek, *Iraq: The Borrowed Kettle* (London
and New York: Verso, 2004), 9–10.

This world of images in which everything can be made to confirm or deny anything is the limit case of a proliferation of a culture of the simulacrum that has been at least latent in the human propensity for producing art objects of all kinds since who knows when, but it has been dramatically speeded up with the invention and rapid extension of reproducible technologies: photograph, film, video, computer. Recall Susan Sontag's claims that photography has done "at least as much to deaden consciousness as to arouse it" and that images circulated without credible explanations are "inexhaustible invitations to deduction, speculation, and fantasy."[14] They are also, as Zeliser and Baudrillard himself have shown in their accounts of the Holocaust photographic archive and of the Timisoara massacre, respectively, raw materials available in the cause of misattribution or sheer deception. It is possible to hold out the hope that the very fungibility of the image, its capacity to mean anything to anyone, may still bespeak a challenging universalism when it represents the evidence of death: the body in the picture may not be who or what it is said to be, but it could be dead and it could be you. There is much that impedes such identification, especially when so many of such images participate in an already familiar and traditionalized vocabulary of death or violence. But there can also be surprises, as there were with the Abu Ghraib photos, which arrayed their individually familiar components (pornography, the funfair, torture, death) into formats that were not familiar, idiosyncratic groupings and that were and continue to be disorderly and challenging. As such they refuse the sublime response that can be derived from a single catastrophic event like the fall of the Twin Towers, and that depends (as Kant long ago made clear) precisely on the beholder's relative distance from its life-threatening physicality and on his or her capacity to restore the briefly interrupted self-control of normal behavior now lifted from the sphere of unconscious habit and made visible as an earned and morally charged equilibrium.

The Abu Ghraib photos offer nearly nothing of that, which is one of the reasons why the effort to blame what they depict on a "few bad eggs" has not been more successful in closing off attention and debate. They break down the otherwise largely intact bound-

14. Sontag, *On Photography*, 21, 23.

aries between them and us, where "them" includes not only the Iraqis suffering the consequences of our invasion but also the troops who are obliged to carry it out, those whose class identities and volunteer status have normally kept from sight the ways in which they are just like everyone else, the rest of us. One might at least imagine that these photos were faked, as was the one that appeared in the London *Daily Mirror* at around the same time. And, as I have said, we live in a world in which the accusation or assumption of faked evidence is almost normative. But no one raised this question about Abu Ghraib or thought about it for very long. The staging of these incidents as pranks rather than as formal spectacles provided exactly the touch of the real that might have been absent from more carefully composed images falling into the inherited genres of wartime reportage. The most common response has not been one of skepticism or fatigue—whereby these images could be anything, or they're already everything and everywhere, and are hence either not true or so true as to be uninteresting—but one of acceptance and difficult recognition. In this respect they stand in for all the images we are not seeing that might have similar effects—not only the other two hundred or so other Abu Ghraib photos withheld from publication but also the evidence of the horrible deaths and disfigurations happening on a daily basis in Iraq. They occupy the place that we are otherwise being aggressively refused: the place of the real.

They take us, in other words, beyond or around the sublime and the spectacular, into some interior zone of ongoing confusion and obscure identification. They do not disprove or discredit the role of the spectacle in the unfolding encounter with death that those in the homeland have been experiencing since 9/11, but they impose an added dimension and demand a different response. Susan Sontag objects to what she takes to be the dominance of Baudrillardian aesthetics in commenting that "to speak of reality becoming a spectacle is a breathtaking provincialism. It universalizes the viewing habits of a small, educated population living in a rich part of the world, where news has been converted into entertainment."[15] The choice is not quite so simple, given that this same small population owns, dominates, or heavily influences the operations of the major media,

15. Sontag, *Regarding the Pain of Others*, 110.

which are themselves actively disseminating a simulacral mentality as widely as they can, and certainly in the rich part of the world, where al Jazeera and other alternatives are not available. But Abu Ghraib really is an alternative. It offers intimacy in the place of distance, involvement instead of observation. It is not the intimacy of language, of the dialogic exchange beloved of so many liberal theorists. Here, inside the prison, the scene of interaction cannot be imagined as an eyeball-to-eyeball battle of wits between interrogator and prisoner, a rule-bound exchange in which internationally sanctioned basic decencies are preserved, in which the conventional humanity of the enemy other is respected and upheld. The turbulent and discordant juxtapositions of leering soldiers and naked prisoners, individually and in piles, speak of a connection more brutal and immediate, a display of violent force that is not directed at eliciting information (most of the detainees did not have any) but at registering the possession of the power of life and death.

Neither the intimate scene of torture nor the spectacle of the falling towers then leaves any room for the Habermasian model of democratic cultures operating at their best—by talking. Habermas, or at least a boiled-down version of Habermas, has been the philosopher of choice for the international neoliberal consensus since the end of the Soviet empire in 1989.[16] His preference for dialogue and the pursuit of rational consensus as the best means of settling political disputes was easily adapted to a victorious Western ideology that attributed its own historical triumph to its possession of these very habits and ideals. Bringing this up himself in the aftermath of 9/11, Habermas repeated what he had said before but said mostly in such a low voice that it had been drowned out by the roar of approbation his more optimistic arguments had given rise to: that the theory of communicative action was always just that, a theory whose effect as an applied method would always depend on circumstances that might, in extreme cases, render it inapplicable. Such an extreme state of affairs, he

---

16. See Žižek, *Welcome to the Desert of the Real*, 122–23, for an account of Habermas's popularity with the prime minister of Spain, the same Aznar who supported the Iraq War by sending Spanish troops and who was dramatically deposed after seeking to pin the Madrid train bombings on his own preferred source of terror, the Basque nationalists. Žižek takes 9/11 to be proof of "the utter impotence of Habermasian ethics" (34).

found, seemed to be in place after 9/11, but not just *because* of 9/11. We can't just blame terrorism. If successful communicative actions require "symmetrical conditions of *mutual* perspective taking," without which there can only be a "spiral of violence" recursively duplicating and intensifying itself, then an appropriate environment can only be imagined as resulting from "the political taming of an unbounded capitalism" without which "the devastating stratification of world society will remain intractable."[17] The terms that dominate the reigning conversation are part of the problem, not the solution. As Ted Honderich puts it: "Nothing calls out for more analysis than talk of *freedom,* unless perhaps it is *the American way of life.*"[18] So too those other terms we have encountered: *Ground Zero, sacred* or *hallowed ground, heroes, axis of evil,* and so on. These terms assume a clear definition in the minds of those who deploy them, but either they register an uncomfortable hyperbole that argues against taking them at face value or they dissolve into oxymoronic formulations inscribing binary antagonisms into the place of entities.

Derrida, who for much of his career had been a target for Habermas and his followers, spoke bluntly, but with a bluntness that is complex, of 9/11 as the symptom of a crisis in the autoimmune system of the West, specifically of a "suicidal autoimmunity" whereby America has itself trained and subsidized the forces that have turned against it. The hijackers thereby incorporate "two suicides in one: their own (and one will remain forever defenseless in the face of a suicidal, autoimmunitary aggression—and that is what terrorizes most) but also the suicide of those who welcomed, armed and trained them."[19] This is, importantly, not new: "one could endlessly multiply examples of these suicidal paradoxes." Not only are the events of Abu Ghraib the events of American prisons, but bin Laden wealth is/was deeply implicated in the U.S. economy, Osama himself was a former ally in the war against the USSR in Afghanistan, Saddam himself was an ally whom America supported in his war against Iran (and who in 1988 gassed some of his own citizens, the Kurds—one of the

17. Borradori, *Philosophy in a Time of Terror,* 35–37.
18. Honderich, *After the Terror,* 180.
19. Borradori, *Philosophy in a Time of Terror,* 95.

crimes produced against him in 2003—with weapons financed by American support). Every imagining of the other is an encounter with the self: *they* are *us*. The phantasm of international terror— everywhere and always, unseen and ready to strike—is the reflection of global capitalism; the fundamentalism of Islamic radicals is the fruit of modernization, not of primitive tradition, just as the crazed figure of Mistah Kurtz is, in both Conrad's novel and Coppola's film, one of our own.[20] The model of autoimmunity is one that had preoccupied Derrida for some time before 9/11. Taking his metaphorical cue from the biological language of the AIDS crisis, he had found in political systems a tendency to create immune and autoimmune components *at the same time:* no immunity without immunity to immunity, in other words. The production of "antibodies against foreign antogens" also incurs acts of "protecting itself against its self-protection."[21] The more defenses one puts up, the more one erodes one's own defenses. By such "strange illogical logic... a living being can spontaneously destroy, in an autonomous fashion, the very thing within it that is supposed to protect it against the other."[22] The more power accruing to a state, the more powerful its autoimmune tendencies become: the exemplary state, the image and agent of the crisis in globalization, was and is the United States.[23]

Derrida's biological paradigm is not instrumentally at odds with the Marxist model devised by Althusser, whereby the relative autonomy of the ideological state apparatuses could provide for an objective display of the processes of class struggle. Behind him there is Marx himself, arguing in *The Eighteenth Brumaire of Louis Bonaparte* that the French bourgeoisie came to understand that "all the weapons which it had forged against feudalism turned their points against itself... all the means of education which it had produced rebelled against its own civilisation," so that "the sword that

20. Here I am drawing on Žižek, *Welcome to the Desert of the Real*, 27, 38, 43.

21. Derrida, *Acts of Religion*, 80. For an application of the model to the European scene, see Jacques Derrida and Elisabeth Roudinesco, *For What Tomorrow . . . A Dialogue*, trans. Jeff Fort (Stanford: Stanford University Press, 2004), 178.

22. Jacques Derrida, *Rogues: Two Essays on Reason*, trans. Pascale-Anne Brault and Michael Naas (Stanford: Stanford University Press, 2005), 123.

23. Jacques Derrida, *Without Alibi*, ed. and trans. Peggy Kamuf (Stanford: Stanford University Press, 2002), 261–62.

is to safeguard it must at the same time be hung over its own head as a sword of Damocles."[24]

One might choose to take this tradition of reflexive reaction, from Marx to Derrida, whereby all attempted damage to or protection against the other is damage to the self, as a sort of wish fulfillment implicit in the reciprocality of the Hegelian master–slave paradigm, a principle of utopian mutuality that renders impermanent all the oppressive power structures in the world. A faith, or a hope perhaps. But one can also recognize its suitability for explaining the empirical conditions of violence and self-protection from violence, most simply visible in the behavior of the state toward its own citizens, whether in the streets of Baghdad or in the implementations of the Patriot Act. Baudrillard also takes up the image of a biological recursiveness from which no one is exempt, seeing the current convulsions as "a fractal war of all cells, all singularities, revolting in the form of antibodies."[25] So internal to our life system is this violence attributed to the other that we ourselves, he suggests, have dreamt of it and predicted it, a fact "which can indeed be measured by the emotive violence of all that has been said and written in the effort to dispel it" (5). Terrorism, like capitalism, is indeed presented to us in the language of cells, networks, clusters, nodes—a cyborg vocabulary that perfectly expresses the melding of biology and information theory that is neither human nor nonhuman but each in the other. We do not see here the unmodified, natural body upon which Eagleton relies to float his model of empathic propriety and the case against theory, but a body form already implicated in world systems. The identification with the other, however, is still proposed and explained. The models of autoimmune crisis (Derrida), of fractals (Baudrillard), and of paranoia (Žižek) all reflect and project what the historical record demonstrates with increasing clarity, even as the political apparatus seeks to obscure it: that they are us and we are them, or, if not quite this (for the suffering is not equal), at least that the principles of identification, actual or potential, are hard to refute and tend in

24. Louis Althusser, *Lenin and Philosophy and Other Essays*, trans. Ben Brewster (New York and London: Monthly Review Press, 1971), 127–86; Karl Marx and Friedrich Engels, *Selected Works*, 3 vols. (Moscow: Progress Publishers, 1973), 1:435–36.

25. Baudrillard, *Spirit of Terrorism*, 12.

the direction of sympathetic coexistence. To inhibit or prevent this, the state ideology requires a strong negation (sometimes called "evil") whose hyperbole draws attention to itself. Abu Ghraib, I have argued, was critical here, the last straw adding to the load of a camel already groaning with the weight of a history of complicity and mutuality. We too are torturers. So too the disposition of terror falls evenly among the Unibomber, Timothy McVeigh, the anthrax terrorist (not yet discovered but apparently one of us), the government executors of the Waco massacre, and Osama bin Laden's jihadists. There is every evidence to support and contribute to theory's emphasis on the self-generated identity of the other and on the reflexivity of a violence that cannot be restricted to one part of the system, as we are promised it might be by the language of revenge, of justice, of good and evil. That identity is also, in its more positive potential, the common identity of the human form and the suffering body, which also must be suppressed if the idea of a war of good against evil is to be maintained.

THEORY AND TERROR

The figure of terror has been with us for a long time and was previously articulated as taking the form of the Russian, the Chinese, the Palestinian, and the Libyan—because terror is itself an abstraction whose empirical location need never be proven and can be projected as existing everywhere. Before that terror was, of course, the privilege of the state itself, whether in Jacobin France in the 1790s or Stalinist Russia in the 1930s. That original formation has never been displaced, only disavowed and displaced. Now terror is once again not just outside but inside the homeland in the form of the sleeper cell as well as in the immune/autoimmune strategies designed to contain it. Hegel's master–slave paradigm reappears in modified form as the democracy–terror syndrome: democracy makes terror in order to consolidate its own identity as unitary and internally consistent. The threat of the sleeper cell, the enemy within, is so radical and so substantially true (it is in all of us) that it has been displaced onto an entirely contingent foreign entity—Iraq. Derrida's now-canonical argument about the function of the Platonic *pharmakon* as neither poison nor cure but always both (with the emphasis a matter of rhetorical or political pressure and not of essential qualities) should further help us keep in mind that the relation between America and its others cannot be understood as that of the pure negation promised by the politicians. In order to explain itself to itself, America needs the un-American, without which it has no meaning. As the defenses of democracy veer between celebration of us (the Freedom Tower) and denigration of the other (once the evil empire, more recently the axis of evil), it is critically important to remember that each identity can only be postulated in terms of the other and as inseparable from the other. But the suffering is, even after 9/11, unequal. Iraqi civilian deaths already massively exceed in numbers those perpetrated by al Qaeda. Our commemoration of the dead has been turned to the production of many more deaths. The innocence of the dead of 9/11, who happened to be on a particular airplane or working in a particular building, has been answered by the infliction of massive casualties on hundreds more of American and thousands of Iraqi bodies, also innocent, and disposed of with impunity: bare lives, squandered to demonstrate that the power of the state remains intact and that the extent of its ability to reduce persons to things, and nothings, remains unassailable. The state of exception invoked to legitimate these practices (just in case there remain any who might demur) is not only a transnational gesture directed at the foreign but an internally punitive principle, as was the "state of siege" (Belagerungszustand) Marx described as imposed on Paris after 1848 and exported "over the whole continent" thereafter, as occasions were made to demand.[26]

The image of Hegel, resurrected by Francis Fukuyama after 1989 as the precursor of the end of history, remains even more powerfully immanent as the explicator of a history that refuses to remain in the past, one that must be repeated and reworked by all modern Western individuals in a process that could be imagined to involve a critical maturation but is just as or even more often one of arrest or fixation: the complex that will not pass through the dialectic but remains forever the shape of our lives. What Hegel in one voice proposed as a passage from feudalism into early modern life, typified by the bringing to consciousness

26. Marx and Engels, *Selected Works*, 1:412.

of the master–slave encounter as a recognition of mutuality (signaling thereby the beginnings of democracy), remains also un-
surpassed and unsurpassable (ontogenetically programmed),
in a world situation wherein one unchallenged great power casts
itself as at once *for* the world and yet something distinctly in and
for itself and for which the world is the other, the enemy. Gil
Anidjar's brilliant and important analysis of the double imperative within the Western ethical inheritance to at once punish the
enemy and love him as oneself, to be and not to be one's own
enemy, tells us that the specific figure of this drama is the Jew
and the Arab, as one, "distinct, but indissociable" as "the condition of religion and politics."[27] Europe (the West) is the kingpin
in the deployment of a figure of the Jew and Arab as interchangeable antagonists, so that no polarization of any two terms
(Europe and the Jew, Europe and the Arab, the Jew and the
Arab) can subsist without the silent and unanalyzed assumption
of the other. This secret sharing is written into the sacred texts
that enjoin us to love our enemies, to beware the friend who is
an enemy, to know our enemy from our friend, all at the same
time, as well as into an extended theological and cultural heritage that Anidjar explains and exposes. It is not so much that circumstances of historical and geographical propinquity render
Jew and Arab identical to the point that only paranoid ideology
can maintain absolute distinctions but that they are in their differences one and the same in the gaze of the West, and as such
the composite figure of an enemy always open to opportunistic
reinvention as the Jew against the Arab or the Arab against the
Jew. The gaze of the West: this is what determines, in its congru-
ence with enormous military and (albeit under stress) economic
power, the instability of all rhetoric of settlement in the Middle
East, all efforts to choose between Jew and Arab as friend and
enemy (so the British were once pro-Arab against Israel as
America is now pro-Israel against the Arab), all efforts to establish either absolute difference or absolute sameness. Behind and
within this syndrome is the common archive of the Abrahamic

27. Anidjar, *The Jew, the Arab*, xi. This book is a compelling exploration and
extension of the work of Derrida, as the author makes clear throughout. See also
Anidjar's introduction to Derrida, *Acts of Religion*, 1–39.

religion wherein Judaism, Islam, and Christianity are all fighting for space and mutual differentiation.[28]

The imagination of terrorism as at once outside and within threatens this effort at differentiation because of its insistence that there are no longer any sure distinctions between the friend and the enemy, the self and the other. The panic is visible in, for example, Alan Dershowitz's assertion that "we must adopt a far more aggressive policy against every nation—friend and foe alike—that lends any support to terrorism."[29] Friend and foe *alike*. If friends are foes then are there any friends?[30] It is visible too in Michael Ignatieff's advice that we have need of the word *evil* as we struggle to make sense of our own proclivity to torture, otherwise we take the risk of failing to distinguish what we do from what "Muslims" do. The word *evil*, applied to them, "holds the line" between them and us, between their implacable cruelty and our historical "capacity for repugnance."[31] Dershowitz's terrorists are like "cunning

28. See Julia Kristeva, *Strangers to Ourselves*, trans. Leon S. Roudiez (New York: Columbia University Press, 1991), 65–76, 84–85; and, of course, Sigmund Freud, *Moses and Monotheism*, trans. Katherine Jones (New York: Vintage Books, 1967), with its analysis of the implications of the idea that Moses was an Egyptian. This extraordinary book, written in the mid to late 1930s "to deny a people the man whom it praises as the greatest of its sons" (3) and "with the audacity of one who has little or nothing to lose" (66), has generated an ongoing debate about homelands and foreigners, identity and difference. See, among others, Yosef Hayim Yerushalmi, *Freud's Moses: Judaism Terminable and Interminable* (New Haven: Yale University Press, 1991); Jacques Derrida, *Archive Fever: A Freudian Impression*, trans. Eric Prenowitz (Chicago: University of Chicago Press, 1996); and Edward W. Said, *Freud and the Non-European* (London and New York: Verso, 2003). Freud addresses the oddity of the injunction to love one's enemy (or neighbor) as oneself, in *Civilization and Its Discontents*, where it is explained as a necessary inhibition on the natural aggressivity of mankind (59–61) and thus a principle of civilization (69) of relatively recent origin (89). See also the important analysis in David L. Clark, "Kant's Aliens: The *Anthropology* and Its Others," *CR: The New Centennial Review* 1, no. 2 (Fall 2001): 201–89.

29. Alan M. Dershowitz, *Why Terrorism Works: Understanding the Threat, Responding to the Challenge* (New Haven: Yale University Press, 2002), 186.

30. Derrida began one of his seminars with an epigraph from Montaigne: "O my friends, there is no friend." See Jacques Derrida, *Politics of Friendship*, trans. George Collins (London and New York: Verso, 1997).

31. Michael Ignatieff, "The Terrorist as Auteur," *New York Times Magazine*, November 14, 2004, 58.

beasts of prey: we cannot reason with them" (182), but they are at the same time invisible within the body of the friendly states and within the homeland. Far from being an exceptional state, torture may then become the normative method for the interpellation of an enemy who is otherwise, except for the dynamic of torture itself, invisible, not open to articulation or representation. Most of those subjected to brutal treatment in the prisons of Iraq, Afghanistan, and even Guantánamo have not been likely sources of important information; they are simply filling a role. They stand for and stand in for an innumerable series of undiscovered figures of terror whose name is legion. Derrida called this "performative interpretation," that which "transforms the very thing it interprets."[32]

I take this term from Derrida's profound and yet-to-be assimilated analysis of the effects of 1989, an event before 9/11 but one that has conditioned the commemorations through which we are still living. After 1989, which was seen to inaugurate a new freedom from the shackles of a contested political legacy established with the French Revolution two hundred years earlier, America and the West found themselves in want of the enemy. The defeat of the Soviet empire was also widely welcomed as the defeat of (what was called) theory: the period of revolutions and international turbulence from 1789 to 1989 was also the time when there flourished an abstract, methodical, and propositional language that described experience as if from a distance and in spite of idiosyncratic variations of the kind beloved of conservative thinkers (also theorists, of course), whether as the rights of man, the new economic plan, or the mathematical array of welfare statistics. No matter that "theory" came to include many and diverse forms of thought, many of which were quite at odds with any leftist or statist ambitions or endorsements: the association of theory with Jacobin politics was polemically set in stone in the 1790s and never fully disestablished.[33] Hence theory has been seen to have come most acutely to the forefront at moments of left-historical crisis: 1789, 1848, 1917, 1968. This is why for *theory* one can so often read *Marx*, why liberalism and capitalism are so seldom imagined as

32. Jacques Derrida, *Specters of Marx: The State of the Debt, the Work of Mourning and the New International,* trans. Peggy Kamuf (New York and London: Routledge, 1994), 51.

33. See David Simpson, *Romanticism, Nationalism, and the Revolt against Theory* (Chicago: University of Chicago Press, 1993).

having a theory at all, and why theory in the universities has almost exclusively been both claimed by and blamed on those who have taken positions against the ruling orthodoxies. Thus it was Marx who was taken up by Derrida, writing after 1989, in response to Marx's projection as the synecdoche of a redundant past by those in the liberal consensus who claimed that now the time of communism and of theory (and also of world conflict) was definitively over. Derrida saw these hyperbolic and strident claims as a "triumphant conjuration" trying to "disavow, and therefore to hide from, the fact that never, never in history has the horizon of the thing whose survival is being celebrated (namely, all the old models of the capitalist and liberal world) been as dark, threatening, and threatened."[34] With what now looks like astonishing prescience, but by way of that which was perhaps evident to him in the aftermath of the first Gulf War, Derrida located as crucial to the coming history the crisis in the Middle East and the war for the "appropriation of Jerusalem" that was being and would be fought all over the world (58). The popular dismissal of Marxism is nothing more or less than the dismissal of the *specter* of Marx, the specter of the communism that figures (*as* a specter) in the first sentence of the *Communist Manifesto*. As such this dismissal is, for all its triumphalism, something impossible and desperate, because the specter is not only the ghost of what has been but the figure of what is always about to return, to revisit and reappear. Its invocation thereby represents "untimeliness and the disadjustment of the contemporary" (99). Here is the opening of Marx and Engels' manifesto: "A spectre is haunting Europe—the spectre of Communism. All the powers of old Europe have entered into a holy alliance to exorcise this spectre: Pope and Czar, Metternich and Guizot, French Radicals and German police-spies."[35] In those days too there was a coalition of the willing, and one considerably more diverse than it is today. But the ghost they were seeking to lay to rest has already generated an indefinite afterlife of reappearances—including, one might note here, the adverse reconjuring of "old Europe" by Donald Rumsfeld (or his theoretically literate speechwriters?), not as the recrudescence of a favored entity but precisely as that which now must be left behind by the new world order.

34. Derrida, *Specters of Marx*, 52.

35. Marx and Engels, *Selected Works*, 1:108.

The figure of haunting and the paradigm of *hauntology* Derrida devised to fit this history perfectly encompass the epistemology of life in the face (but there is no face) of terrorism: "The subject that haunts is not identifiable, one cannot see, localize, fix any form, one cannot decide between hallucination and perception, there are only displacements; one feels oneself looked at by what one cannot see."[36] So too the Jew (and the communist) in the Nazi state, everywhere and nowhere; so too the reds under the bed in the manufactured U.S. cold war imagination. Are we not indeed once again terrified (which means being told that we should be terrified) by that which we cannot see? Agency here is no simple matter; we feel ourselves looked at both by the covert gaze of the terrorist and by the seeing eye of the national surveillance system designed to protect us *against* terrorism, which is always open to implantation as its avowed opposite, the panoptical state. The West, wanting an enemy, imagines one everywhere, inspiring a state of constant vigilance inside and outside borders that are no longer efficient. In so doing it terrorizes its own population. The taking down of barriers that is the hallmark of neoliberalism's conquest of the globe (walls, tariffs, borders) also encourages the conjuring up of enemy agents circulating uncontrollably through the new body politic. The homeland has been there before, in the red-baiting years of the cold war, with the largely show trials and investigations mimicking in the free world exactly what was condemned in the totalitarian states. Now the stakes are higher and the window of response critically briefer: we have (again Dershowitz is the bellwether) "an endless war with ever changing enemies, always moving from place to place."[37] In both Europe and the United States, the opening of borders has induced a heightened paranoia about immigration, even as immigration is absolutely essential to the functioning of all sectors of the homeland economy, from the agricultural workers and janitors to the high-technology specialists. Friends and enemies are everywhere, and no one can be sure which is which. The role of the state and its spokespersons is thus to simplify the task and to tell us.

This paranoia perhaps partly explains the credibility achieved, against all empirical evidence, by the Bush and Blair administra-

---

36. Derrida, *Specters of Marx*, 136.
37. Dershowitz, *Why Terrorism Works*, 6.

tions in their demonization of Saddam's Iraq as the primary source of evil in the world after 9/11. The panic at the shapelessness of the enemy–friend legitimates his strong localization as primary enemy in a convenient place whose significations are overdetermined by various contingent rationalizations (the need for oil, the spread of democracy, the finishing of the job begun in 1991, and so forth). So it was Iraq that was chosen as a simple space–time location at which to claim to fight the war against terror. Did anyone seriously entertain the idea that every able-bodied terrorist would flock to Baghdad in order to show up at Armageddon? One of the subsidiary justifications for the invasion of Iraq (and there were *only* subsidiary justifications) claimed precisely this, that fighting in Iraq would preempt fighting in the homeland, would "finish the job." This justification does not contradict the other claim that this is an endless war to be fought everywhere; it is its supplement and its double. The war is both everywhere and in one place, and both at once. The panic at imagining terror without a definite profile is assuaged by calling it Iraq. What is missing, in both senses of the term, are the faces of the dead and maimed Iraqis who happen to live there.

The specter of terror has taken the place of the specter of communism, and it sits on the back of another massive "disadjustment of the contemporary" (Derrida's account of the force of the specter) effected by the fall of the Twin Towers and announced as such by the apologists of apocalypse. In this strong disadjustment, all sorts of fantasies and projections become marketable, including that of the localized responsibility of Iraq for the disaster of 9/11 and the image of an enemy who is or could be everywhere or anywhere. The response of the Bush-Blair administrations and their favored or sponsored intellectuals has been coercive and dangerously overconfident. The foreign and other spokespersons for "theory" have generally done better. The commitment to a thoroughgoing dialectical analysis wherein no entity is allowed to stand free of identification with its other leads to an ethics, aptly summarized by Žižek, wherein "the only appropriate stance is unconditional solidarity with *all* victims."[38] This perception means we cannot allow ourselves to be browbeaten into refusing to ask why 9/11 is worth so

38. Žižek, *Welcome to the Desert of the Real*, 51.

much more attention than the massacres of Hutus, Kurds, East Timorese, and a host of others in recent and current history (127). Hume's claim that we naturally tend to feel more sympathy for persons who belong to the same subgroup as we do (the nation, for example) will not satisfy an ethical instinct that sees this statement as the problem rather than the solution. Similarly, when we are required to choose for or against terrorism, for or against America, the West, democracy, Žižek is right to remind us that *precisely in such moments of apparent clarity of choice, mystification is total*" (54).[39] The absolute decision imagined in such a choice bears no relation to the lives that almost everyone in the homeland leads: the capacity for damage possessed by terrorists has empirically been *always* limited. The events of 9/11 have not yet really changed the high degree of relative security enjoyed by almost all of us in the employed middle class almost all of the time. There is for most of us no likely point in our lives at which we will ever have to be *for* or *against* the West, terror, or democracy in any way that is not simply rhetorical or ideological. To project this kind of imaginary choice of self on a largely inert and secure population is deceitful and pseudo-empowering (remember the recruiting poster: "The best weapon against terrorism . . . You"). It has been principally deployed to justify illegal detentions and random violence against civilians of the wrong color or in the wrong place at the wrong time.

THE TORTURED STATE OF ETHICS

We have never left the domain of ethics. It is now time to encounter it more frontally. A great deal has been written by ethical-legal scholars and commentators on the implications of 9/11 and our responses to it for civil rights, for the criminal justice system, and for the ethical justification of democracy. The invasion of Iraq itself was after all legitimated as a response to an ethical imperative, bringing freedom from tyranny, from threat, from the prospect of mass destruction. Everything from voting rights and the rights of women and freedom of speech and movement to economic

---

39. Even Derrida, in an uncharacteristic concession, speculates about what he might do "if I had to take one of the two sides and choose in a binary situation"; see Borradori, *Philosophy in a Time of Terror,* 113.

prosperity, education, and religious toleration was being promised as the result of America's military occupation of Iraq. *They* were going to be able to be like *us*. Such high-pitched rhetoric required wholesale recourse to the language of ethical integrity. Michael Ignatieff, one of the most widely quoted among the house liberals who justified the invasion on human rights grounds, replicates even in his later admission of error the very phenomenon that so beguiled him in the first place. Admitting, after Abu Ghraib and much else, to the dangers of defending a culture like ours that has made "a civil religion out of its self-belief," and owning up to the egg on his face at the subsequent evolution of the war and the occupation he himself supported, he yet consoles himself with the saving observation that we did "one thing well," we "overthrew a dictator." The rest, finally, is up to them: "America cannot defend Iraq from its demons of division: it can only help Iraqis do so."[40]

What is the ethical texture of a position like this? What is its logic and what assumptions does it depend on? The desperate desire to make the best of things (I cannot help recalling the song from Robert Altman's bicentennial movie of 1976, *Nashville*, the one whose refrain is "We must be doing something right to last two hundred years") supposes that the removal of a "dictator" is an indisputable good, without asking us to question what a dictator is and whether Saddam was obviously first in line for this humane intervention. It also assumes, with reckless complacency, that there is an "Iraq" that simply has to pick itself up and make itself anew, as opposed to, for example, an already fragile agglomeration of ethnicities, religions, and interests originally gerrymandered into statehood by the British, suffering since 1991 from the effects of American-imposed economic embargoes, and now shattered beyond recognition. Demons of division are somehow the property and the fault of the Iraqis: there is no acceptance of the possibility that those divisions have been created or at least manipulated by outside interests (the West) during the entire history of this place called "Iraq," and that the prospects for any disinterested future involvement are minimal without the sort of radical change in the hearts and minds of Americans and their allies.

40. Michael Ignatieff, "Mirage in the Desert," *New York Times Magazine,* June 27, 2004, sec. 6, p. 16.

Ignatieff's language here, precisely because it ingratiatingly makes an admission of limited error, is symptomatic of a deep problem with the rhetoric of justification and its indifference to any fully dialectical interrelation of them and us, not only in the empirical record (which this author certainly knows well) but also in the very habit of thought and expression that allows him to deploy entities such as *dictator* and *Iraq* not only as self-evident things in themselves but as things unconnected to us and our histories. It would be hard to defend the idea that Saddam was any sort of enlightened despot, though it is important to know that he has been seen that way among the supporters of secular Arabism. But the use of the word *dictator,* all on its own, establishes a radical distinction between him and us that covers over the history whereby we have (as in many other instances) kept him in his place, funded him, supported him, and turned a blind eye to a series of violent acts whose coincidence with our own interests has led us to suppress rather than encourage critique. This means that the history of foreign policy is *not* the history of a concern for human rights; the language of human rights is available when it suits us to employ it for some other purpose. In his most recent book, Ignatieff sees his job as nothing less than "to help citizens and leaders make the hazardous choices that a successful struggle against terrorism requires."[41] The task is all about *us;* the world after 9/11 is going to test the integrity of our democracy, our human rights claims, our legal apparatus. Again there is the language of anguish: *our* security requires that we sometimes do things that go against *our* laws and values. There is a "moral risk" (12) here, he admits, that cannot be avoided and that should be faced. Hence the book's title, *Lesser Evil,* which raises the question of "what lesser evils may a society commit when it believes it faces the greater evil of its own destruction?" (1).[42] Let us stop right here. Has our society reached this point? Is there or has there even been any serious evidence that "we" face "our" destruction in some wholesale way? There has not and there is not, and further on in his book Ignatieff says as much (54ff.).

41. Ignatieff, *Lesser Evil,* vii.

42. One exemplary albeit extreme precursor of this recently popular "lesser evil" argument is Himmler's notorious Posen speech of 1943, in which the moral repugnance of what had to be done in the name of the fatherland (and for the sake of its survival) was fully articulated but only to add to the dignity of the perpetrators.

Looking again at the opening sentence, we must then ask what might be the force of the strange disclaimer whereby what matters is whether a society *believes* that it faces its own destruction. Are we to assume that the same terms of inquiry and the same conclusions govern a society that *is* facing its own destruction (for example, Russia invaded by Germany in 1941) and one that merely *believes* it to be the case? And if America after 9/11 might be described as a society of the second sort, one that believes in its own imminent destruction, *who* is the society, who makes up and speaks for the *it?* What sense can be made of a sentence aspiring to ethical argument which includes as a qualifier the words "when it *believes* it faces the greater evil of its own destruction"? In the days after 9/11 was I alone in thinking that the prospects for a massive attack on the homeland were close to zero? There were many others who thought the same. So what is morally and legally admissible in the way of lesser evils for a society (that is, its leaders) that *believes* but is not sure it is about to be destroyed? A society that perhaps has absolutely no hard evidence it is about to be destroyed?

The efforts to rationalize a way through this uncertain and unmeasurable gap between what we know and what we think we might find out have led, notoriously, to a recrudescence of intellectual legitimations for torture. The most well-inspected effort at justifying torture under strictly observed limits has come from Alan Dershowitz in *Why Terrorism Works* (131–63), which took up the "extraordinarily rare situation of the ticking bomb terrorist"—the person who has vital information that would save lives but only if it were delivered in critical time–because he found that in Israel this instance was being used as a generic example to uphold a *system* of "coercive interrogation," which he describes in the same paragraph both as "the use of torture" and something that "bordered on" torture in general (140–41). Dershowitz proposes that if judicial warrants for nonlethal torture were available under extreme (and only extreme) circumstances, like that of the ticking bomb terrorist, then the actual incidence of under-the-radar torture might decline radically. His is an interesting and challenging case, superficially appealing in its declared good intentions and its faith in the power of an educated bureaucracy. It does, however, invite objections concerning its prospective implementations. The ticking bomb terrorist syndrome assumes a situation of panic, uncertainty, and haste, one in which it would be practically impossible to be sure who is and is not a candidate for torture, and in which there would certainly be no time to go up a chain of command for exact legal review and authorization. What does one do–torture everyone? Does the calculus of possible gain extend to the innocents rounded up along the way who *might* be ticking bomb cases? If so, how many? And if not, how would one know in advance that the one person one targets is the right person, since by definition we do not have the information that would convict him or her? Suppose we suspect that someone might be a ticking bomb case but we are not sure? The whole equation assumes that we know in advance what we want to apply torture to find out–that the suspect is the right person. Furthermore, the presence of the judicial warrant on the books, the climate of interrogation created by such knowledge, already puts on the table the credibility of torture and thus leads every interrogator to worry that he or she is missing the person who requires it. The empirical paucity of cases in which the ticking bomb syndrome has been seen to apply (apparently only one in Israel after all these years) makes the case even less applicable to real-life situations. And what, in reality, would the experience of being the torturer do to the interrogator, whether he gets it right or gets it wrong?

Examples such as that of the ticking bomb terrorist are of course infinitely fascinating as thought experiments, of the sort beloved of law school and government school graduate seminars, and therein perhaps lies the danger of academic legitimations of political actions of the sort that have parlayed the commemoration of 9/11 into the invasion of Iraq. Michael Ignatieff's *The Lesser Evil* rehearses and rejects the case for torture (133–44), but only in the context of a larger argument for tolerating the lesser evil by way of an "ethics of prudence" (9) governed by "actions in defense of democracy which will stray from democracy's own foundational commitments to dignity" (8), actions that might, in the minds of others, easily come to include the use of limited torture that is, for this author, beyond the limit. One can agree that the world would be a better place if Ignatieff's recommended requirements for the use of force were met: stringent adversarial review, sunset clauses, maximum transparency of evidence and legislation. But unless the conditions of our (frequently manufactured) *belief* in our insecurity are critically examined, then the "ethics of prudence" risks functioning simply as an opportunity for politicians to invoke academic justification ("well, we have permission from Harvard's Human Rights Center to incur the lesser evil") for behavior motivated by things quite other than democratic convictions. (It might also function to gather and focus a constitutional opposition to the current practices, it should be said.) It is here that issues around the media, ideology, and culture at large crop up, and it is here that the traditions of theory have much to offer. Take the following statements by Ignatieff:

> A lesser evil morality is antiperfectionist in its assumptions. It accepts as inevitable that it is not always possible to save human beings from harm without killing other human beings.

and:

> It is tempting to suppose that moral life can avoid this slope [i.e., getting it wrong] simply by avoiding evil means altogether. But no such angelic option may exist. Either we fight evil with evil or we succumb.[43]

We are accustomed to hearing people claim credit for not being perfectionists, for understanding the pressures of the real world, in the service of all sorts of devious intentions. But what real-life situations are implied here, and for whom? Who have we been killing to save others from harm, and what was the harm? Does this formulation apply to those unnecessarily dead Iraqis, mostly civilians? Does it protect the United States, or are we assuming that we are acting on behalf of those other Iraqis who are at least for the time being still alive? What is the evil that we must fight or else be overcome by? Who is in a position to overcome us? If these are real-life occasions, then what are they? I think they are dangerously abstract projections, "what if" scenarios of the sort so beloved of liberal moral theorists as they imagine themselves in existentially fraught moments of decision that for most of them (us), most of the time, *never* occur. We are thus preparing ourselves in the imagination for clear-cut moral choices that never in fact

43. Ignatieff, *Lesser Evil*, 21, 19.

present themselves simply as moral choices. On the very rare occasions that these dilemmas occur outside the classroom, they would be contextualized by various kinds of information, pressures from various interests, probability calculations that affect the nature of the action meditated. Suppose the dilemma is about torture. Do we have the right person? If so, will torture tell us what we want to know? Is the probability or likelihood of success sufficient to even meditate this action? The evidence suggests that torture has seldom been the outcome of these sorts of rational deliberations. The typical torture scene is routinized violence directed at whoever happens to be vulnerable, a gesture that has little to do with information and a great deal to do with power, prejudice, display, and the pornographic imagination. To imagine the torturer as a conscience-stricken democrat with the fate of others at his fingertips is a grotesque heroization of a much grubbier reality of the sort on view at Abu Ghraib and in many of America's prisons.

Ignatieff, as I have said, does not condone torture. But the articulation of the "lesser evil" scenario has the dangerous potential to become a school-of-government version of the fairy tales and romances that insulated the young Wordsworth from throwing up at the sight of the drowned man of Esthwaite. The hypothetical ethically prudent legislator or interrogator, when faced with a situation he does not fully understand or control, where information is lacking and consequences unclear, can bring to mind his education in the "lesser evil" argument and go right ahead with the assurance that he has been prepared for just this eventuality. The advance preparation in the mind actually then risks having the torturer (or politician, or bomber pilot, or tank commander; again, Ignatieff himself does not condone torture) imagine that the scene is simpler and clearer than it is, and above all it tells him that the scene is manageable albeit difficult, that there are precedents, that a larger benefit is at stake. He may thus be creating a situation that can be subsequently defended and justified but that has little or nothing to do with the victim or his or her circumstances. The imaginary predicament of the heroic torture scene, with the fate of others (even nations) hanging in the balance (the ticking bomb syndrome), then comes to be transplanted into the more mundane brutalities of combat and prison culture. The moral risk here is not just that the torturer or politician can get it wrong. The risk is that the epistemological and evidentiary clarity that would at best be required for any punitive behavior ever to be justified is hopelessly compromised by a rhetoric of urgency that is finally going to be in almost every case a projection of mere belief. Or worse yet, that what will be invoked by way of excuse as a *belief* is really a composite of fear, sadistic cruelty, indecision, mere obedience, and an inability to *suspend* belief itself. A culture in which the other is regularly demonized, in which we are constantly bidden to accept the need to fight evil with evil, in which we are told that you have to take the risk of hanging or torturing the wrong man unless we are all going to go down the tubes, is a culture to be feared and resisted on every available front.

After all of this, one last sentence from *The Lesser Evil:* "Only in liberal societies have people believed that the pain and suffering involved in depriving people of their liberty must make us think twice about imposing this constraint even on those who justly deserve it" (17). In other words, we feel their pain but not enough to stop us from inflicting it. With a U.S. prison population at record levels, it is good to know that society is (or has been?) thinking twice. The claim seems to be that imperfect as we are, we are still the best thing on offer. I suppose we, at least some in the homeland, are at the moment thinking twice about, for example, the death penalty, though not hard enough to get rid of it. This defense of liberalism does not sit comfortably in an argument about lesser evils: it can only serve to give confidence to those readers imagining themselves as making the critical decisions; it tells them that the cause in which they are bombing or torturing is the best cause there is, at precisely the moment when the maximum degree of circumspection seems to be required and called for.

The way of thinking that Michael Ignatieff's book represents, with its base in liberal individualism and recourse to the constitution, is flawed not only in its indifference to, for example, economic injustice as a critical part of any context for "lesser evil" arguments, but also in its lack of awareness of what both history and theory have had to say about the permeability of the crucial boundaries between self and other. A full recognition of these contributions would not just add to the debate but would refigure it completely. Liberals should worry not only about the propriety of violently punishing people but about how they decide on those who "justly deserve it." Before we accede to the self-righteous application of the massive force we possess (similar to what Auden memorably called "the conscious acceptance of guilt in the fact of murder"),[44] before we accede to the pertinence of the "lesser evil" argument put forth in Ignatieff's book, we must hope that there might be space and time for an ethics not hopelessly reified by abstractions, by pieties about the sanctity of liberalism, by an unearned level of comfort about locating evil and making distinctions between us and them. And if there is hope, then what politics might come from or along with it?

There is hope. Abu Ghraib holds a lesson that many already know and others are becoming dimly aware of: that if you are given the job of a prison guard, you are at risk of becoming a torturer; and that if or when you do, you will be giving way to instincts, pressures, and desires that have little to do with a classroom exercise in the "lesser evil" conundrum. Abu Ghraib, as I have argued in chapter 3, puts us in the position of the torturers in uncomfortable and challenging ways that have less to do with calculations about relative degrees of doing good or doing harm than with an awareness of the vulnerable bodies of both prisoners and guards. It is difficult to set limits on the scope and effect of these identifications and distancings, and *that* is what is important about the photos: they cannot be closed off, although the powers that be are doing their best to move us along to some happier topic. They certainly cannot be handled by the sort of rhetoric on display in Ignatieff's book, which adopts the "bad apples" position in declaring that a democracy must enforce its rules by "dismissing from service any of the carnivores who disgrace the society they are charged to protect."[45] Abu Ghraib put some real flesh on the old adage about forms of civilization being always also forms of barbarism, and not just in the reductive sense that one man's culture is another's primitive society. Chris Hedges' powerful book *War Is a Force That Gives Us Meaning* makes the point that unspeakable cruelties occur in all wars, and he tells us about some of them in almost unbearable detail. These things tend to happen when communal ties and patterns of culture are

44. *The English Auden: Poems, Essays, and Dramatic Writings, 1927–39*, ed. Edward Mendelson (New York: Random House, 1977), 212.

45. Ignatieff, *Lesser Evil*, 144.

broken down or exploited by politicians or profiteers with some vested interest at stake, and who turn to patriotism or nationalism to disguise what they are doing. Intellectuals and journalists are perhaps more than usually prone to buy into these gestures in that they are, as Hedges puts it, "willing to line up behind leaders they despise in times of national crisis" (48). Speaking of the first Gulf War, which he witnessed, Hedges remarks that "the press wanted to be used. It saw itself as part of the war effort" (143). Who can forget the droves of academics and intellectuals who were jostling to be first in line to testify, after 9/11, of their shock and outrage and their renewed commitment to what they called America? Many have fallen silent since those heady days, but the time for reflection and understanding has barely begun, not least because it has had to respond to a national climate of war and violence first in Afghanistan (which has now as good as disappeared from the news) and then in Iraq.

Some of the most powerful moments in Michael Moore's *Fahrenheit 9/11,* along with the footage of the dead and dying, are the interviews with the ordinary Americans in uniform who have seen firsthand the way that killing happens and who are understandably distressed by having to do it and to risk their own lives along the way. The historical evidence for the theoretical conviction of the immanent togetherness of them and us, the subject and its other, could hardly be more eloquently presented. So too Sergeant Pogorny, whose story was retold in chapter 3. One inevitable feature of this intimate alliance between friend and enemy shows up in the aftermath of these conflicts, not just in the phenomenon of postcombat stress disorder (why is it a *disorder?* Why is it not the expectation?) but in the physical damages imposed on the subjects in the homeland–the wounds, the artificial limbs, the reactions to their own weapons (Agent Orange in Vietnam, depleted uranium in 1991, who knows what in 2003). As these and other such phenomena pass into the common culture, it becomes clear that the compassion for all victims everywhere that Žižek proposed is not only a desirable ethics but a prospect for experiencing everyday life. Drawing on Hegel and Levinas among others, along with her experience of the AIDS epidemic and its human and political outcomes, Judith Butler has begun the task of exploring our "fundamental dependency on anonymous others" and on the "precariousness of

life" as an analytical model for the critique of a culture wherein the
high ground of compassion has for some time been occupied by an
untheorized or "antitheory" philosophical establishment operating
in the confidence that it can tell us how to relate to the other without hearing what the other might say or think or feel.[46] Her thesis
supplies a psychoanalytic explanation of some of the phenomena
I have been describing: she proposes that our expressions of grief
are in fact expressions of a "disavowed mourning" whereby only
some are mourned while others are ignored (xiv), and that what
results is a situation requiring that the "narcissistic preoccupation of
melancholia" resulting from this impeded mourning be "moved
into a consideration of the vulnerability of others" (30). She notes,
for example, the exclusion of any specific mention in the various
obituaries and memorials that appeared of the queer lives lost on
September 11, 2001 (35). Starting right there, with those eerily
formulaic obituaries published as the "Portraits of Grief," I have
argued that one can see the profile of a compression of significant
attention that presented the victims themselves almost as if they
had been already dead (the photos, the perfectly shaped lives, the
lives that were almost all the same). The Taylorization of mourning
has not stopped. It is apparent in the debates about the future of the
World Trade Center site, in the fuss over *Nightline* and the coffins of
the dead soldiers at Dover Air Force base, in the nearly complete
silence about the non-American dead in Iraq and elsewhere.

Abu Ghraib provides an opening, and I have been affirming that
what is called theory (imaged as foreign, systematic, dialectical)
offers us a language for developing and understanding the experience of torture and witnessing torture, though certainly not for laying it to rest. I began this chapter by asking questions about the
suitability and legitimacy of speaking of theory *in the time of death,*
and I contested Eagleton's assertion that disavowal of the body and
of mortality was precisely theory's problem and limitation. My
response is and has been that theory has been intensely preoccupied with death, even to the point of obsession, and that Eagleton is
wrong to reify it as that which avoids an engagement with matters
of life and death. What we call theory was certainly, in the later

46. Judith Butler, *Precarious Life: The Powers of Mourning and Violence* (New York
and London: Verso, 2004), xii, xvii.

1960s, making claims for a liberating and rejuvenating energy attending the death of the subject, the death of the author, and the release into language, into *text* and *writing,* as beyond institutional containment and suggestive of a political future briefly thought by some to be visible in the historical form of Maoism. But even then the sense of darkness and constraint was never fully absent, most visibly in the outright critiques of the student movement by the radicals of an early generation–Althusser, Adorno–but also in the more stringent methodological reservations of Derrida, Foucault, and others about the impossibility of escaping the determinations of the only language one has at hand for thinking in, a language already employed and deployed in rigid institutional formations, already enshrined in the dead letter. For this reason what was to come was seldom if ever promised in the form of a return to Eden or a restitution of intact forms of life; it would appear instead as "an absolute danger . . . as a sort of monstrosity."[47] This now reads as eerily prescient of the same language of apocalypse that would resurface after 9/11 and which had indeed, as Derrida would himself come to show, been ready at hand for the European reception of the "red specter" that Marx projected onto the scene of modernity. The form of monstrosity has not yet been fixed, and it has taken some time for the most enduring theories of the 1960s to settle into even the beginnings of a settled reception or understanding. The best of them have called and still call for urgent revisiting in the light of subsequent crises of both representation and interpretation, which is to say politics. Very little here is out of date; much has yet to find its readers or its moment on the stage.

That said, the mood and message of much of theory since the golden age of the late 1960s have been downbeat: the grim rigor of an ideology critique that seemed to argue chiefly for the difficulty or impossibility of nonrevolutionary change at a time when revolution itself seemed to be no longer believable. Theory has grown in other directions, of course: into an impassioned and still ongoing call for an end to various tyrannies of race and gender, into a demand for a tolerance and recognition of the non-Western other, even into a rejigged defense of the liberating potential of

47. Jacques Derrida, *Of Grammatology,* trans. Gayatri Chakravorty Spivak (Baltimore: Johns Hopkins University Press, 1976), 5.

desire. Definite kinds of social progress can be attached to (if never simply attributed to) and articulated by what we call theory. But theory has also directed its attentions to the shadows cast by Auschwitz, the name whose invocation stands for a range of brutalities and a number of unnecessary deaths whose extent is, without such nominalist economy, seemingly impossible to express. The conjunction of theory with death is then not just another example of the rhetorical flattening and nationalistic self-regard of which the event of 9/11 has already been used to sponsor far too much; we are not simply colluding in the state of mind that thinks that just because death has come home to us on such a scale and in such an unexpected way, then the whole metaphysical and methodological imagination of the rest of the world is supposed to experience a radical transformation. The transformation had already occurred, and the project of theory was already embedded within it. This situation has produced some notorious one-liners, or lines that have been taken as such, lines such as Adorno's "to write poetry after Auschwitz is barbaric" and "all post-Auschwitz culture, including its critique, is garbage."[48] But the reiterated circulation of such statements is merely a brief synopsis or aide-mémoire of what has not been forgotten, what has been constantly subject to an effort to commemorate, though not at the same time in all places: Adorno was writing these things in the late 1940s, long before the victorious anglophone states turned their collective attentions in the same direction. The United Nations has recently introduced Holocaust Remembrance Day, an idea that has massive support for a whole range of reasons, not all of them admirable. This will be the latest in a series of commemorations that have preoccupied the mass media as well as the critical and historical academy in the West for a good many years: it too requires the attentions of theory.

Among the many meanings and connotations that Auschwitz attracts to itself or has had thrust upon it, there is that of the foreigner, the enemy, the other, about which I have already spoken in

48. Theodor W. Adorno, "Cultural Criticism and Society," in *Can One Live after Auschwitz? A Philosophical Reader,* ed. Rolf Tiedemann (Stanford: Stanford University Press, 2003), 162; idem, *Negative Dialectics,* trans. E. B. Ashton (New York: Continuum, 1973), 367.

the spirit and the wake of Derrida, and of the tradition he so magisterially embodies. Marx, our proxy for theory, had for Derrida best remain always a foreigner, a specter who has once been but is yet to come, "a glorious, scared, accursed but still a clandestine immigrant as he was all his life."[49] Marx the uncanny, the unhomely; Marx the sleeper cell. After 1989, Derrida projected the increasing instability and permeability of all boundaries and borders—between states, between the living and the dead (169), between human and animal (85)—and a reciprocal counterprojection of disenfranchised persons—exiles, homeless and stateless people, immigrants (81)—as part of the effort at maintaining the old orders of business. Adorno again had proposed, in 1951, the same year as Heidegger's lecture on dwelling discussed in chapter 2, that "dwelling, in the proper sense, is now impossible" and that (going well beyond Heidegger here) "it is part of morality not to be at home in one's home."[50] More recently, and with massive attention from theorists in the academy and some beyond, Giorgio Agamben has proposed that the "refugee is perhaps the only thinkable figure for the people of our time and the only category in which one may see today . . . the forms and limits of a coming political community."[51] This entails the giving up of "naive notions of the citizen and a people" (18) and insists on "a renewal of categories that can no longer be delayed" (23). Under the terms of the status quo, the power of the state has made the state of exception into the rule: "power no longer has today any form of legitimation other than emergency, and . . . everywhere and continuously refers and appeals to emergency as well as laboring secretly to produce it" (6). I have suggested already the striking suitability of Agamben's paradigm for an understanding of the commemorative culture of the United States after 9/11 as it re-created the very categories under threat (those portrayed in "Portraits of Grief," all of whom were made into exemplary "citizens") and projected an exemplary enemy/other/foreigner who was at once territorialized (Afghanistan, Iraq) and imagined everywhere, even within the homeland. The suspension

49. Derrida, *Specters of Marx*, 174.

50. Adorno, *Can One Live after Auschwitz?* 40, 41.

51. Giorgio Agamben, *Means without End: Notes on Politics*, trans. Vincenzo Binetti and Cesare Casarino (Minneapolis: University of Minnesota Press, 2000), 16.

of rights and conventions and the arbitrary disposition of life and death (not only with the smartest of weapons) worked to shore up the image of an intact state that did indeed feel itself (was felt by its rulers) to be under threat. Adorno's caveat came to be reversed, and the portentous history behind its articulation came once again to mind: now it was important to assign morality exclusively to being at home in one's home. It is enormously important, if anything is important, to resist this imperative both as empirical description (for this is not how it is for many persons) and as ethical injunction. Primo Levi has written of how, even in that most bounded of environments that was Auschwitz, there was a coming and going of goods carried by those few who were in a position to come and go: the boundaries of the camp that were so tragically absolute for so many human lives were not devoid of an "economic life," a mediated connection with the outside.[52] The most consciously carceral of environments has its leakages, and they are planned as such as the very means of its maintenance. So much more permeable are the borders of states that do not think of themselves as carceral but that cannot fully confront the openness their own ideologies avow as all important.

DER MUSELMANN

Both the image of Auschwitz and the terms of our encounter with vulnerability and violence, with the enemy other, are incisively focused in another of Agamben's books, one that offers us some important lessons and also some important cautionary lessons—*Remnants of Auschwitz*. As I have said, while much of theory can be located within the time of death, Auschwitz has become emblematic in a way that Treblinka or Belsen or other places have not, partly because it was the most fully conceived and complex of the Nazi concentration camps, with a semipermanent society of transient prisoners whose bodies were disposed across various sites for labor, execution, further shipment, and mere survival. Unlike those places where Jews and others were simply shoved out of trains or vans and shot or gassed immediately, Auschwitz had a

---

52. Primo Levi, *Survival in Auschwitz: The Nazi Assault on Humanity,* trans. Stuart Woolf (New York: Simon and Schuster, 1996), 82.

culture (in the neutral sense of the term: a habit-formed way of life through time, albeit tragically brief for most of its inhabitants), and one fully integrated into the labor cycle and the cycle of life and death. At Auschwitz, for those who made it through the selections, there was time, though precious little of it. And time produces culture, however minimal. The disposal of bare life by the Nazi state was most dramatic at those places where no one survived. From thence there are no memoirs. Auschwitz, with its investment in a hideously refracted image of the factory system as productive of other things besides corpses, put itself on semipermanent display. It can be and has been commemorated.

Agamben's distinctions between ethical and juridical categories, and his attention to the ways in which the latter tend to condition or preempt the former—so that the law is interested in judgment "independent of truth and justice"—are of great value for anyone trying to think through the judicial responses to what is called terror, especially in a world where judgment is compulsively legitimated by reference to truth and justice.[53] One would not think of Auschwitz as an instance of the operations of an autoimmune crisis, in which the system somehow attacks its own protective mechanisms. There seems little if anything of a utopian potential at work here. The phenomenon of the *Sonderkommando*, those who were made to empty the gas chambers, sort the bodies, and run the crematoria, is a powerful and troubling instance of the manipulated synthesis of self and other. Those whose bodies one handles are one's fellow prisoners, fellow Jews, perhaps one's friends and relatives. They are also one's own imminent future. Nazi torturers (for is this not torture?) made prisoners dig their own graves, bury their own children or parents, experience in life the full abjection of the deaths of others as their own death. The selves that are harmed are not however those of the Nazi overseers. They set things up to refuse any identification with the bodies they were destroying, forcing this work on the prisoners themselves, and thereby they brought about the very identification of the Jew as subhuman that had been the avowed justification for the genocide itself. In other words, they themselves created what they claimed to find in place. Agamben proposes that people did not

53. Giorgio Agamben, *Remnants of Auschwitz: The Witness and the Archive,* trans. Daniel Heller-Roazen (New York: Zone Books, 2002), 18.

die in Auschwitz: "the Being of death is inaccessible and men do not die, but are instead produced as corpses" (75). But the most striking and provocative element of Agamben's account is, for my topic here, the story of the *Muselmann*. According to the author this subject has hardly been touched: he finds only one extended, published study (55). The Muselmann, as readers of Levi and Bettelheim will know, is the shadowy, liminal figure of the prisoner near death, or at least almost out of life, showing no emotion or response, drifting aimlessly and wordlessly around the camp, the lowest form of human life that can still be called human. He is "the threshold between the human and the inhuman" (55) and thus also "the guard on the threshold of a new ethics, an ethics of a form of life that begins where dignity ends" (69). For those still working and functioning in some nonminimal way, he is a guarantee of their relative prosperity, a sign that they can yet fall much farther than they have so far. He assures their own humanity in a world in which almost nothing else does. There are very few images of these figures (50–51): no one wants to see them, and no one who survived wants to remember them. As they gave other prisoners some temporary sense of relative well-being, so they also represented what most of the others would become, the living dead.

When one goes, however, to the accounts of the Muselmann that Agamben reprints in an appendix (166–71), something different appears, something beyond the narrative he has so far given us. There are indeed the memories of those survivors who found these figures inert, without emotion, speechless, beyond rescue. But there are also memories of others who helped them, who picked them up when they fell, who gave them food. And most remarkably, there are the memories of others who were themselves *Muselmänner,* who survived to tell their stories against the grain of Agamben's theory and of some of the testimonies that they were beyond life, about to die.[54] Not only do these figures beyond speech now speak, but they tell of what they felt–the overpowering desire for food, the dreaming of bread and soup, the rummaging in the trash for anything that could be eaten. There is, or was, in other

---

54. Dominick LaCapra notes the same disjunction, in *History in Transit,* 175–77. His account is, as I have said, a significant counterstatement to various of Agamben's claims and assumptions.

words, no clear division between the Muselmann and the other prisoners, no point at which *they* were wholly different from *us*, the rest. (I am assuming that we identify with the observers and not—yet—with the Muselmann as we read the descriptions on the record.) They too had desires they could act on or dream about; they too took part in minimal social exchanges, touching and even speaking. The dichotomy that some in the camp appear to have maintained was to a degree constructed: the living dead were made to seem liminal or subhuman and then shunned or feared because of it. Perhaps they had given up, but so too had those who called them and made them—*Muslim*. Because that is, of course, the translation of *Muselmann*, and it should give us pause for thought. What does it mean that a Jew near death should call another Jew nearer death a Muslim? This question goes oddly undiscussed by Agamben. The origin of the term is, he claims, unsettled (see 44–46), but we know that part of what it means is non-Jewish, other to the Jew. You who were Jewish are now, as the sign of your passage into the inhuman, to be called Muslim! We also know, after Derrida and Anidjar's work, that the Jew really is, historically, at one with the Muslim in the eye of the European beholder.[55] So the Jew of Auschwitz is and is not the Muslim, and under the stress of Auschwitz he accedes to the nomination of himself as the other; in German, the language of the dominators, he recognizes and repeats the conjunction. In this way he replicates an entire history whereby, in the foundational political economies of the eighteenth century, the Jew and the Arab are gathered together as both the victims and the worthy objects of despotism—those who are culturally already signified by a resignation that is then reduplicated by the power of tyranny: resignation brutally imposed on the already resigned. They are rendered supine, passive, without the will to change, the will to live for themselves or live at all, and because they are already like that, no crime is involved. For Montesquieu, for Hegel, the Jew and the Arab overlap under the umbrella of an oriental passivity.[56] After World War II, Primo Levi encounters and

55. Anidjar, *The Jew, the Arab*, 113–49, gives the most thorough account of this "figure of absolute abjection" (119), the Muselmann, that I have seen. See also his comments in Derrida, *Acts of Religion*, 17–20.

56. Anidjar, *The Jew, the Arab*, 125–29.

seeks to resist a "commonplace still prevailing in Italy" that the Jew is "humiliated," one who "tolerated centuries of persecution without ever fighting back"[57]—just like the Muslim, the icon of resignation, another icon now being so aggressively challenged by the suicide bombers, beheaders, and militant jihadists in the Middle East. That this resignation is also a powerful component of Christian doctrine of course renders this act of abjecting the Jew and the Muslim as all the more paranoid.[58]

Levi's story is one of survival, of course, and of resistance in various subtle forms, but it is also, between the lines, a recognition of the status of *all* of the inmates of Auschwitz as *Muselmänner*, since to outsiders all of them are "untouchables" (120), all "worthy of the unarmed death which awaits us" (150), all "starving spectres . . . greyish skeleton bones in rags" (161). The Jew is the Muslim. Beyond the camp, and into the everyday world, Freud had proposed for the melancholic individual, Jew or not, a similar result, not enforced by cruelty, starvation, and humiliation but stimulated by the thwarting of the mourning process, an "extraordinary diminution in his self-regard . . . an overcoming of the instinct which compels every living thing to cling to life."[59] Does it reduce and profane the phenomenon of the Muselmann for us to wonder whether the circle of inclusion is getting wider and wider, like that of Agamben's refugee, image of bare life, of the coming community, joining the ranks of those whom Derrida too saw proliferating beyond number: "never before, in absolute figures, never have so many men, women and children been subjugated, starved, or exterminated on the earth"?[60] As with all powerful metaphors for a predicament sensed as general, there is a risk, a risk of profanation, of opportunism. But there is also a positive potential, of the kind that Agamben appeals to under the name of an ethics. The Jew

57. Levi, *Survival in Auschwitz*, 185–86.

58. The supposed tendency of the Jews to resignation has created not only the mythology of Jewish nonresistance to the genocide (despite the Warsaw uprising and rebellions in various camps) but also the assumption that no one talked about the Holocaust until the 1970s.

59. Sigmund Freud, "Mourning and Melancholia," in *The Standard Edition of the Complete Psychological Works of Sigmund Freud*, ed. and trans. James Strachey and Anna Freud (London: Hogarth Press, 1957), 14:246.

60. Derrida, *Specters of Marx*, 85.

who called his other self the Muslim did so in the language of the tyrant, the German, *Muselmann:* "I do not know why," says Levi (88). Who knows what depths of irony, desperate humor, or other associations might have governed the idiom of the camp? (Why were the sorting sheds called *Kanada?*) The Muslims, writes Levi, are those who "do not begin to learn German," who are the "backbone of the camp," the "anonymous mass . . . already too empty to really suffer" (90). The Jew who speaks the language of the European can interpellate the Arab (other) Jew as Muselmann, but he endorses the terms of an abjection that can and likely will become his own, as it already has in the eyes of the outsider. He is already the Arab Jew. This breaking down of the effort at distinction undercuts the intended self-securing of the German-speaking Jew, the effort to pretend that he can be at home. And as the circle extends outward, as more and more people stand to be included in the category of the defiled, those who can be killed with impunity, so the antagonism between the power of the state and the wellbeing of most persons becomes larger and larger.

Agamben's account does not mention the bizarre present-day resonances of the Muselmann paradigm, nor does it therefore fully explore its potential. For if the Muslim really is a Jew, and if in fact (if the printed memories are to be trusted) many other prisoners really did not ignore but assisted or engaged with the Muslims, who were themselves, moreover, at least occasionally *not* beyond the realm of the living (because some of them survived), then the binary distinction Jew–Muslim does not hold up in the face of what occurred even in Auschwitz. This is *not* then a form of life "where dignity ends" (69), though it clearly seemed that way to some. I prefer to see in the quiet words, the scraps of food, and the occasional helping hand that passed between the Jew and the Muslim, the German and the non-German speaker, a shared sense of the vulnerable body that speaks for a different kind of dignity. One cannot of course propose that such limited experiences should be a working norm for those of us comfortably ensconced in other and happier lives. But the theatricality of the Auschwitz idiom could serve to remind us that Israel, for example, is really Israel-Palestine and always has been; that Iraq is not very far from Lower Manhattan; that to propose, as many in the homeland did, that 9/11 was a shock to the *world* and not just to America involves

taking seriously what that world is and how its parts hang together.)
It has been widely recognized that 9/11 was remarkable as a world
event and that it was witnessed on television, often in real time, all
over the world. And to a remarkable degree the sight of those
falling towers, the fates of those who died, and the grief of those
who survived elicited a worldwide outpouring of sympathy and
response that was clearly announced and reported. Could this have
been a utopian moment, an opening? Was it genuine, and does it
matter?

If we follow Baudrillard then the spectacular nature of the 9/11
disaster seems to make it implausible to speak here of the *genuine*.
Similar worldwide responses were generated by the reporting of
Princess Diana's death. Suppose it is just the fact of celebrity itself
and the potential for journalistic epitome presented by a disaster
like a car crash or the fall of mighty towers that best explains why
so many become so involved? What distinguishes such events
from, say, the long wars or famines that have occurred all over the
world in the same years but that are much harder for the media to
keep before us (assuming they choose to represent them at all) by
way of an efficient array of manageable and repeatable images?[61]
Is this also what has assisted the Abu Ghraib photos in their continuing existence as worldwide focus points? (Is it the celebrity status of the United States) in the imaginary lives of so much of the
media-connected world that makes *its* tragedies so much more
compelling than those of other less visible nations, so that to offer
or experience sympathy with the victims of 9/11 is to fantasize
about being American or at one with America in a manner that
shrinks geographical and even economic distance? Perhaps the
United States is collectively what Princess Diana was individually:
an object of impossible privilege and fantasy identification whose
experience of simple mortality is shocking and irresistibly compelling? Or is there a positive potential, empirical or utopian, in
this sight of ordinary people and ordinary grief experienced amid
enormous cultural, economic, political, and military power, as
Ariel Dorfman thought there was in the common recourse of survivors all over the world to appearing with photographs of their
dead?

61. On this topic, see Moeller, *Compassion Fatigue*.

If so, if there was on September 12, 2001, and for some time thereafter such a potential for the making of common cause, has it been lost forever by the invasion of Iraq and the ongoing brutalities it has perpetrated on both the enemy and the homeland? Has the nationalization of commemoration, so aggressively withheld from the enemy other (the Arab who may also be the Jew), ruined once and for all any prospect for cultivating an active sense of the demise of those whose suffering and dying bodies are not American (which requires also the repression of the physical destruction of those who are)? The effort that has been put into this is strenuous and has been relentless: the imaging of the World Trade Center dead as a microcosm of the homeland; the planning of the Freedom Tower and its accompanying buildings; the withholding of any public encounter with our own dead soldiers; the repression of any sustained sight of the death and destruction they have wrought and are (at considerable human cost to themselves) still wreaking with tanks and bombs and weapons smart and not so smart; and the persistence, almost to the point of hysteria, of an asserted absolute distinction between democracy (or freedom) and terror. But this effort has not been seamless or wholly efficient. Abu Ghraib set in motion a process of interference and interrogation of the self–other, homeland–foreigner binary that at the time of writing has not ceased, as it continues to associate itself with countless other sites in Iraq, in the countries to which prisoners have been "rendered" (sent for unmonitored interrogation), in Guantánamo, and in the homelands themselves: Deepcut barracks in England, where four army recruits died in apparent suicides and where over a hundred allegations of abuse, some amounting to torture, have been lodged; or the U.S. prison system and its analogues in rogue police departments, where persons have died in detention or in public beatings. No simple or tidy distinction between us and them, between the homeland and the other place, the place of the enemy and the foreigner (which has also been the place of theory), can now be sustained without the massive avoidances and cover-ups that we still see but that are wearing thinner and thinner. Simple dwelling in the homeland is no longer conceivable for anyone who pays critical attention to what has been happening; it should now indeed have become "part of morality not to be at home in one's home," as Adorno claimed it was in

1951.[62] In welcoming attendees at the commemoration of the life of Emmanuel Levinas, Derrida spoke of the "violence of the host," whereby "to dare to say welcome is perhaps to insinuate that one is at home here, that one knows what it means to be at home . . . *welcoming* the other in order to appropriate for oneself a place and then speak the language of hospitality."[63] Derrida's work on hospitality should be required reading for those monitoring and manipulating the condition of crisis after 9/11.[64] Can the host of nations, the United States, those within it and in charge of administering it, afford to imagine itself as not in place, as aggressively depriving others of their places in order to shore up the image of the integrity of its own, its right to remain the world's host, giving and demanding hospitality as it sees fit to a smaller and smaller group of the deserving and the willing? Can those who kill with impunity, under the rubric of hypercautionary attention, smartness, clinical precision—which lasts only until the first homeland victim is claimed—ever imagine themselves in the places of their victims? We know that some of them can and have done, including many of those on the front line, those who have witnessed violent death and have realized that it makes no distinctions. We have also seen the immanence of a bleaker and terrifying tendency, one that many had forgotten, so that they allowed themselves to be surprised at its unignorable appearance. Here is that tendency in the words of the main protagonist of J. M. Coetzee's most recent novel: "our compassion is very thinly spread. Beneath it is a more primitive attitude. The prisoner of war does not belong to our tribe. We can do what we want with him. We can sacrifice him to our gods. We can cut his throat, tear out his heart, throw him on the fire. There are no laws when it comes to prisoners of war."[65] This would be an uncomfortable admission to have to make for any culture that projects itself as ethically demanding and strenuously self-monitoring. Perhaps in order to displace the choice be-

62. Adorno, *Can One Live after Auschwitz?* 41.

63. Jacques Derrida, *Adieu to Emmanuel Levinas,* trans. Pascale-Anne Brault and Michael Naas (Stanford: Stanford University Press, 1999), 15–16.

64. See, for example, Jacques Derrida, *Of Hospitality: Anne Dufourmontelle Invites Jacques Derrida to Respond,* trans. Rachel Bowlby (Stanford: Stanford University Press, 2000); and "Hospitality," in Derrida, *Acts of Religion,* 358–420.

65. J. M. Coetzee, *Elizabeth Costello* (New York: Viking, 2003), 104.

tween approving the tearing out of hearts and pondering some radical pacificism as a means to avoid the sight of death, the latest U.S. Defense Department fantasy is wrapped up with robots. The so-called Future Combat System promises to be the biggest military contract in American history. Robots don't get hungry or require retirement benefits and, according to one Pentagon appointee, "they're not afraid . . . they don't care if the guy next to them has just been shot."[66] So far the prototypes have been expensive failures, but this may not stop a project whose incentives are palpable for a society anxious to assure what the same Pentagon spokesperson describes as "combat without casualties"—on his side. When wars and invasions are carried out by robots, then encounters like that of Sergeant Pogorny with the vulnerable body of the enemy will become increasingly rare. Rarer still will be the sympathetic response he experienced. The robotic language of U.S. military endeavors—from Rolling Thunder (Vietnam), Urgent Fury (Grenada), and Just Cause (Panama) to Desert Storm, Shock and Awe, and Enduring Freedom—is already in place: it awaits only the robots to operate its missions.

There will be fewer if any American bodies to smuggle home in coffins and hide under the cloak of decency when robots carry out the project of policing the world and disseminating death. When all the avoidable deaths are the deaths of others, the utopian moment that 9/11 and Abu Ghraib might have sponsored—a moment for radically refiguring the relations of the homeland to the foreigner—will be harder to replicate. We will have arrived at that chilling moment prefigured in the Christian scriptures, the moment that causes the commentators such trouble, the moment that is traditionally taken as figurative or, perhaps, as an instance of the negative demise of the old Jewish law: I mean the moment when Jesus responds to the young man who wants to attend to his father's burial with the implacable sentence, "let the dead bury their dead" (Matt. 8:22; Luke 9:60). The task of preaching the new law overrules the customs of the old, erases its culture of commemoration.

When the tribe of the West conducts its military escapades with robots, we may look back almost with nostalgia to the present age,

---

66. See Tim Weiner, "A New Model Army Soldier Rolls Closer to the Battlefield," *New York Times*, February 16, 2005, A1, C4.

even though, in the wake of 9/11, commemoration has been hijacked by revenge, there has been a visibly commodified national mourning, the image of death has been taken over by the image of falling towers, and those who are still dying accrue no images. The time *is* out of joint, which means that we must work all the harder to find its history and to dispel its mysteries. The time to come is unimaginable if we do not.

Bibliography

"Abu Ghraib, Stonewalled." *New York Times,* June 30, 2004, A22.

Addario, Lynsey, and Johnny Dwyer. "The Wounded." *New York Times Magazine,* March 27, 2005, 24–29.

Adorno, Theodor W. *Can One Live after Auschwitz? A Philosophical Reader.* Ed. Rolf Tiedemann. Trans. Rodney Livingstone and others. Stanford: Stanford University Press, 2003.

———. *Negative Dialectics.* Trans. E. B. Ashton. New York: Continuum, 1973.

Agamben, Giorgio. *Homo Sacer: Sovereign Power and Bare Life.* Trans. Daniel Heller-Roazen. Stanford: Stanford University Press, 1998.

———. *Means without End: Notes on Politics.* Trans. Vincenzo Binetti and Cesare Casarino. Minneapolis: University of Minnesota Press, 2000.

———. *Remnants of Auschwitz: The Witness and the Archive.* Trans. Daniel Heller-Roazen. New York: Zone Books, 2002.

———. *State of Exception.* Trans. Kevin Attell. Chicago: University of Chicago Press, 2005.

Althusser, Louis. *Lenin and Philosophy and Other Essays.* Trans. Ben Brewster. New York and London: Monthly Review Press, 1971.

"Among the Missing." *New York Times,* October 14, 2001, WK12.

Anderson, Benedict. *Imagined Communities: Reflections on the Origins and Spread of Nationalism.* Rev. ed. London and New York: Verso, 1991.

Anidjar, Gil. *The Jew, the Arab: A History of the Enemy.* Stanford: Stanford University Press, 2003.

Auden, W. H. *The English Auden: Poems, Essays, and Dramatic Writings, 1927–39.* Ed. Edward Mendelson. New York: Random House, 1977.

Badiou, Alain. *Infinite Thought: Truth and the Return of Philosophy.* Trans. and ed. Oliver Feltham and Justin Clemens. London and New York: Continuum, 2003.

Barthes, Roland. *Camera Lucida: Reflections on Photography.* Trans. Richard Howard. New York: Hill and Wang, 1981.

———. *The Eiffel Tower and Other Mythologies*. Trans. Richard Howard. Berkeley and Los Angeles: University of California Press, 1997.

Baudrillard, Jean. *The Gulf War Did Not Take Place*. Trans. Paul Patton. Bloomington and Indianapolis: Indiana University Press, 1995.

———. *The Illusion of the End*. Trans. Chris Turner. Stanford: Stanford University Press, 1994.

———. *The Spirit of Terrorism and Requiem for the Twin Towers*. Trans. Chris Turner. London and New York: Verso, 2002.

Baum, Dan. "The Price of Valor." *New Yorker*, July 12 and 19, 2004, 44–52.

———. "Two Soldiers: How the Dead Come Home." *New Yorker*, August 9and16, 2004, 76–85.

Benjamin, Walter. *The Arcades Project*. Trans. Howard Eiland and Kevin McLaughlin. Cambridge: Harvard University Press, 1999.

———. *Selected Writings*, vol. 3: *1935–38*. Ed. Howard Eiland and Michael Jennings. Cambridge: Harvard University Press, 2002.

Bloch, Ernst, Theodor Adorno, Walter Benjamin, Bertolt Brecht, and Georg Lukács. *Aesthetics and Politics*. With an afterword by Fredric Jameson. London: Verso, 1977.

Borradori, Giovanna, ed. *Philosophy in a Time of Terror: Dialogues with Jürgen Habermas and Jacques Derrida*. Chicago: University of Chicago Press, 2003.

Bowden, Mark. "The Dark Art of Interrogation." *Atlantic Monthly*, October 2003, 51–56.

Boxer, Sarah. "Torture Incarnate, and Propped on a Pedestal." *New York Times*, June 13, 2004, WK14.

Brison, Susan J. "Torture, or `Good Old American Pornography'?" *Chronicle of Higher Education*, June 4, 2004, B10.

Butler, Judith. *Precarious Life: The Powers of Mourning and Violence*. New York and London: Verso, 2004.

Butler, Judith, John Guillory, and Kendall Thomas, eds. *What's Left of Theory? New Work on the Politics of Literary Theory*. New York and London: Routledge, 2000.

Chomsky, Noam. *9/11*. New York: Seven Stories Press, 2002.

———. *Power and Terror: Post 9/11 Talks and Interviews*. Ed. John Junkerman and Takei Masakazu. New York and Tokyo: Seven Stories Press and Little More, 2003.

Clark, David L. "Kant's Aliens: The *Anthropology* and Its Others." *CR: The New Centennial Review* 1, no. 2 (Fall 2001): 201–89.

Coetzee, J. M. *Elizabeth Costello*. New York: Viking, 2003.

Culler, Jonathan, and Kevin Lamb, eds. *Just Being Difficult? Academic Writing in the Public Sphere*. Stanford: Stanford University Press, 2003.

Danner, Mark. *Torture and Truth: America, Abu Ghraib, and the War on Terror*. New York: NYREV Inc., 2004.

Dean, Carolyn J. *The Fragility of Empathy after the Holocaust*. Ithaca, NY: Cornell University Press, 2004.

De Quincey, Thomas. *The Collected Works of Thomas De Quincey*. 14 vols. Ed. David Masson. Edinburgh: Adam and Charles Black, 1890.

————. *De Quincey as Critic*. Ed. John E. Jordan. London and Boston: Routledge and Kegan Paul, 1973.

Derrida, Jacques. *Acts of Religion*. Ed. and with an introduction by Gil Anidjar. New York and London: Routledge, 2002.

————. *Adieu to Emmanuel Levinas*. Trans. Pascale-Anne Brault and Michael Naas. Stanford: Stanford University Press, 1999.

————. *Archive Fever: A Freudian Impression*. Trans. Eric Prenowitz. Chicago: University of Chicago Press, 1996.

————. *Of Grammatology*. Trans. Gayatri Chakravorty Spivak. Baltimore: Johns Hopkins University Press, 1976.

————. *Of Hospitality: Anne Dufourmontelle Invites Jacques Derrida to Respond*. Trans. Rachel Bowlby. Stanford: Stanford University Press, 2000.

————. *Politics of Friendship*. Trans. George Collins. London and New York: Verso, 1997.

————. *Rogues: Two Essays on Reason*. Trans. Pascale-Anne Brault and Michael Naas. Stanford: Stanford University Press, 2005.

————. *Specters of Marx: The State of the Debt, the Work of Mourning and the New International*. Trans. Peggy Kamuf. New York and London: Routledge, 1994.

————. *Without Alibi*. Ed. and trans. Peggy Kamuf. Stanford: Stanford University Press, 2002.

Derrida, Jacques, and Elizabeth Roudinesco. *For What Tomorrow . . . A Dialogue*. Trans. Jeff Fort. Stanford: Stanford University Press, 2004.

Dershowitz, Alan M. *Why Terrorism Works: Understanding the Threat, Responding to the Challenge*. New Haven: Yale University Press, 2002.

Dorfman, Ariel. "The True `Desaparecidos.'" *Chronicle of Higher Education*, September 5, 2003, B9.

Dunlap, David W. "1,776 Foot Design Is Unveiled for World Trade Center Tower." *New York Times*, December 20, 2003, A1, A16.

Dwyer, Jim, and Kevin Flynn. *102 Minutes: The Untold Story of the Fight to Survive Inside the Twin Towers*. New York: Henry Holt/Times Books, 2005.

Dwyer, Jim, Eric Lipton, Kevin Flynn, James Glanz, and Ford Fessenden. "Fighting to Live as the Towers Died." *New York Times*, May 26, 2002, A1, 22–23.

Eagleton, Terry. *After Theory*. London: Allen Lane, 2003.

————. *Sweet Violence: The Idea of the Tragic*. Oxford: Blackwell, 2002.

Eakin, Emily. "The Latest Theory Is That Theory Doesn't Matter." *New York Times*, April 19, 2003, A 17.

Edkins, Jenny. *Trauma and the Memory of Politics*. Cambridge: Cambridge University Press, 2003.

Emsley, Clive. *British Society and the French Wars, 1793–1815*. London: Macmillan, 1979.

Filkins, Dexter. "In Falluja, Young Marines Saw the Savagery of an Urban War." *New York Times*, November 21, 2004, A1, 14.

First Annual State of the Mall Report. October 14, 2002. www.savethemall.org.

Foster, Hal. "In New York." *London Review of Books*, March 20, 2003.

Freud, Sigmund. *Civilization and Its Discontents*. Ed. and trans. James Strachey. New York: W. W. Norton, 1962.

———. *Moses and Monotheism*. Trans. Katherine Jones. New York: Vintage Books, 1967.

———. "Mourning and Melancholia." In *The Standard Edition of the Complete Psychological Works of Sigmund Freud*, ed. and trans. James Strachey and Anna Freud, 14:243–58. London: Hogarth Press, 1957.

Friedman, Thomas L. *Searching for the Roots of 9/11*. Discovery Channel, March 26, 2003.

Gettleman, Jeffrey. "Soldier Accused as Coward Says He Is Guilty Only of Panic Attack." *New York Times*, November 6 2003, A14.

Goldberger, Paul. *Up from Zero: Politics, Architecture and the Rebuilding of New York*. New York: Random House, 2004.

Greenberg, Karen J., and Joshua L. Dratel. *The Torture Papers: The Road to Abu Ghraib*. Cambridge: Cambridge University Press, 2005.

Griswold, Charles L. "The Vietnam Veteran's Memorial and the Washington Mall: Philosophical Thoughts on Political Iconography." *Critical Inquiry* 12, no. 4 (Summer 1986): 688–719.

Guterman, Lila. "Lost Count." *Chronicle of Higher Education*, February 4, 2005, A10–13.

Harries, Karsten. *The Ethical Function of Architecture*. Cambridge: MIT Press, 1997.

Harrison, Robert Pogue. *The Dominion of the Dead*. Chicago: University of Chicago Press, 2003.

Hass, Kristin Ann. *Carried to the Wall: American Memory and the Vietnam Veterans Memorial*. Berkeley and Los Angeles: University of California Press, 1998.

Hawkins, Peter S. "Naming Names: The Art of Memory and the NAMES Project AIDS Quilt." *Critical Inquiry* 19, no. 4 (Summer 1993): 752–79.

Hawthorne, Christopher. "Living with Our Mistake." *Slate*, February 25, 2003.

Hedges, Chris. *War Is a Force That Gives Us Meaning*. New York: Public Affairs/Perseus Books, 2002.

Hegel, G. W. F. *Philosophy of Mind*. Trans. William Wallace and A. V. Miller. Oxford: Clarendon Press, 1971.

Heidegger, Martin. *Poetry, Language, Thought*. Trans. Albert Hofstadter. New York: Harper and Row, 1975.

Herder, Johann Gottfried von. *Reflections on the Philosophy of the History of Mankind*. Ed. Frank E. Manuel. Chicago: University of Chicago Press, 1968.

Honderich, Ted. *After the Terror*. Rev. ed. Montreal and Kingston: McGill-Queen's University Press, 2003.

Horkheimer, Max, and Theodor W. Adorno. *Dialectic of Enlightenment*. Trans. John Cumming. New York: Continuum, 1968.

Huyssen, Andreas. *Present Pasts: Urban Palimpsests and the Politics of Memory*. Stanford: Stanford University Press, 2003.

———. *Twilight Memories: Marking Time in a Culture of Amnesia*. New York and London: Routledge, 1995.

Hynes, Samuel. *The Soldiers' Tale: Bearing Witness to Modern War*. New York: Viking, 1997.

Ignatieff, Michael. *The Lesser Evil: Political Ethics in an Age of Terror*. Princeton: Princeton University Press, 2004.

———. "Mirage in the Desert." *New York Times Magazine,* June 27, 2004, 16.

———. "The Terrorist as Auteur." *New York Times Magazine,* November 12, 2004, 58.

Janofsky, Michael. "Redefining the Front Lines in Reversing War's Toll." *New York Times,* June 21, 2004, A1, 14.

Jones, Joseph. "Hail Fredonia!" *American Speech* 9 (1934): 12–17.

Kimmelman, Michael. "Finding Comfort in the Safety of Names." *New York Times,* August 31, 2003, sec. 2, pp. 1, 22.

Koselleck, Reinhart. *The Practice of Conceptual History: Timing History, Spacing Concepts.* Trans. Todd Samuel Presner, Kerstin Behnke, and Jobst Welge. Stanford: Stanford University Press, 1992.

Kristeva, Julia. *Strangers to Ourselves.* Trans. Leon S. Roudiez. New York: Columbia University Press, 1991.

LaCapra, Dominick. *History and Memory after Auschwitz.* Ithaca, NY: Cornell University Press, 1998.

———. *History in Transit: Experience, Identity, Critical Theory.* Ithaca, NY: Cornell University Press, 2004.

———. *Representing the Holocaust: History, Theory, Trauma.* Ithaca, NY: Cornell University Press, 1994.

Langeweische, William. "American Ground: Unbuilding the World Trade Center." *Atlantic Monthly,* July/August 2002, 50.

Laqueur, Thomas W. "Memory and Naming in the Great War." In *Commemorations: The Politics of National Identity,* ed. John R. Gillis, 151–67. Princeton: Princeton University Press, 1994.

Lentricchia, Frank, and Jody McAuliffe. *Crimes of Art and Terror.* Chicago: University of Chicago Press, 2003.

Levi, Primo. *Survival in Auschwitz: The Nazi Assault on Humanity.* Trans. Stuart Woolf. New York: Simon and Schuster, 1996.

Libeskind, Daniel, with Sarah Crichton. *Breaking Ground: Adventures in Life and Architecture.* New York: Riverhead/Penguin Books, 2004.

Lin, Maya. "Making the Memorial." *New York Review of Books* 47, no. 14, November 2, 2000, 33–34.

Lincoln, Bruce. *Holy Terrors: Thinking about Religion after September 11.* Chicago: University of Chicago Press, 2003.

Linenthal, Edward T. *Sacred Ground: Americans and Their Battlefields.* 2nd ed. Urbana: University of Illinois Press, 1993.

———. *The Unfinished Bombing: Oklahoma City in American Memory.* New York and Oxford: Oxford University Press, 2001.

Lukács, Georg. *The Historical Novel.* Trans. Hannah Mitchell and Stanley Mitchell. Lincoln: University of Nebraska Press, 1983.

Marx, Karl, and Friedrich Engels. *Selected Works.* 3 vols. Moscow: Progress Publishers, 1973.

Mitchell, W. J. T. "Criticism and Crisis." *Critical Inquiry* 28, no. 2 (Winter 2002): 567–72.

———. "Echoes of a Christian Symbol." *Chicago Tribune,* June 27, 2004.

———. *Picture Theory: Essays on Verbal and Visual Representation*. Chicago: University of Chicago Press, 1994.

Moeller, Susan D. *Compassion Fatigue: How the Media Sells Disease, Famine, War and Death*. New York and London: Routledge, 1999.

Muschamp, Herbert. "Balancing Reason and Emotion in Twin Tower Void." *New York Times*, February 6, 2003, E1.

———. "Ground Zero Rethought, with Judgment Deferred." *New York Times*, September 18, 2003, C13.

———. "One Vision: A Hill of Green at Ground Zero." *New York Times*, September 11, 2003, B1.

Nakamura, Ellen. "Slow Homecoming for America's Dead." *Guardian Weekly*, May 13–19, 2004, 36.

Nelson, Robert S., and Margaret Olin, eds. *Monuments and Memory, Made and Unmade*. Chicago: University of Chicago Press, 2003.

Nietzsche, Friedrich. *Untimely Meditations*. Trans. R. J. Hollingdale. Cambridge: Cambridge University Press, 1987.

The 9/11 Commission Report, Including Executive Summary. Official government ed. Reprint. Baton Rouge: Claitor Publishing, 2004.

Noble, Phillip. *Sixteen Acres: Architecture and the Outrageous Struggle for the Future of Ground Zero*. New York: Henry Holt, 2005.

Nora, Pierre. *Realms of Memory: Rethinking the French Past*, vol. 1: *Conflicts and Divisions*. Ed. Lawrence D. Kritzman. Trans. Arthur Goldhammer. New York: Columbia University Press, 1996.

Novick, Peter. *The Holocaust in American Life*. Boston: Houghton Mifflin, 1999.

Nudelman, Franny. *John Brown's Body: Slavery, Violence and the Culture of War*. Chapel Hill: University of North Carolina Press, 2004.

Nussbaum, Martha C. *Love's Knowledge: Essays on Philosophy and Literature*. New York: Oxford University Press, 1990.

———. *Poetic Justice: The Literary Imagination and Public Life*. Boston: Beacon Press, 1995.

———. *Upheavals of Thought: The Intelligence of Emotions*. Cambridge: Cambridge University Press, 2001.

Pogrebin, Robin. "Freedom Center Is Still a Somewhat Vague Notion." *New York Times*, June 24, 2004, B1.

Portraits, 9/11/01: The Collected "Portraits of Grief" from the New York Times. With a foreword by Howell Raines and introduction by Janny Scott. New York: Henry Holt/Times Books, 2002; 2nd ed., 2003.

Purdy, Jedediah. *For Common Things: Irony, Trust and Commitment in America Today*. New York: Random House, 1999.

Raines, Howell. "My Times." *Atlantic Monthly*, May 2004, 49–81.

Ricoeur, Paul. *Memory, History, Forgetting*. Trans. Kathleen Blamey and David Pellauer. Chicago: University of Chicago Press, 2004.

Rose, Jacqueline. "Deadly Embrace." *London Review of Books*, November 4, 2004, 21.

"The Roster of the Dead." *New York Times*, September 9, 2004, A22–24.

Rothstein, Edward. "An Appraisal." *New York Times,* October 11, 2004, B1, 7.

Said, Edward W. *Freud and the Non-European.* London and New York: Verso, 2003.

———. *Humanism and Democratic Criticism.* New York: Columbia University Press, 2004.

Scarry, Elaine. *The Body in Pain: The Making and Unmaking of the World.* New York and Oxford: Oxford University Press, 1985.

Sebald. W. G. *Austerlitz.* Trans. Anthea Bell. New York: Random House, 2001.

———. *Campo Santo.* Trans. Anthea Bell. New York: Random House, 2005.

———. *On The Natural History of Destruction.* Trans. Anthea Bell. New York: Random House, 2003.

Shaw, Phillip. *Waterloo and the Romantic Imagination.* Basingstoke, UK: Palgrave Macmillan, 2002.

Simpson, David. "Naming the Dead." *London Review of Books,* November 15, 2001.

———. *Romanticism, Nationalism, and the Revolt against Theory.* Chicago: University of Chicago Press, 1993.

———. *Situatedness; or Why We Keep Saying Where We're Coming From.* Durham, NC: Duke University Press.

———. *Wordsworth and the Figurings of the Real.* London: Macmillan, 1982.

Sontag, Susan. *On Photography.* New York: Farrar, Straus and Giroux, 1990.

———. *Regarding the Pain of Others.* New York: Farrar, Straus and Giroux, 2003.

———. "Regarding the Torture of Others." *New York Times Magazine,* May 23, 2004, 27.

Spiegelman, Art. *In The Shadow of No Towers.* New York: Pantheon, 2004.

Thackeray, William Makepeace [Michelangelo Titmarsh]. "Little Sketches and Roadside Travels: Waterloo: No. III." *Fraser's Magazine for Town and Country* 31 (1845), 94–96.

"The Times and Iraq." *New York Times,* May 26, 2004, A10.

Venturi, Robert, Denise Scott Brown, and Steven Izenour. *Learning from Las Vegas: The Forgotten Symbolism of Architectural Form.* Cambridge: MIT Press, 1997.

Weiner, Tim. "A New Model Army Soldier Rolls Closer to the Battlefield." *New York Times,* February 16, 2005, A1, C4.

Wiener, Robert. *Live from Baghdad: Gathering News at Ground Zero.* New York: Doubleday, 1992.

Winter, Jay. *Sites of Memory, Sites of Mourning: The Great War in European Cultural History.* Cambridge: Cambridge University Press, 1995.

Wordsworth, William. *The Prelude; 1799, 1805, 1850.* Ed. Jonathan Wordsworth, M. H. Abrams, and Stephen Gill. New York: W. W. Norton, 1979.

———. *The Prose Works of William Wordsworth.* 3 vols. Ed. W. J. B. Owen and Jane Worthington Smyser. Oxford: Clarendon Press, 1974.

www.arlingtoncemetery.com/contents.htm.

www.greatbuildings.com/buildings/World_Trade_Center.html.

www.oklahomacitynationalmemorial.org.

www.wtcsitememorial.org.

Yerushalmi, Yosef Hayim. *Freud's Moses: Judaism Terminable and Interminable.* New Haven: Yale University Press, 1991.

———. *Zakhor: Jewish History and Jewish Memory.* Seattle: University of Washington Press, 1982.

Young, James E. *At Memory's Edge: After-Images of the Holocaust in Contemporary Art and Architecture.* New Haven: Yale University Press, 2000.

———. *The Texture of Memory: Holocaust Memorials and Meaning.* New Haven: Yale University Press, 1993.

Zelizer, Barbie. *Remembering to Forget: Holocaust Memory through the Camera's Eye.* Chicago: University of Chicago Press, 1998.

Zernike, Kate. "Prison Mistreatment." *New York Times,* August 4, 2004, A8.

Žižek, Slavoj. *Iraq: The Borrowed Kettle.* London and New York: Verso, 2004.

———. *Welcome to the Desert of the Real.* London and New York: Verso, 2002.

Index